Thank you for picking up my book. Your support means a lot, and I hope you find the read both enjoyable and insightful. Beyond being an author, my work extends into research and consultancy within organizational behavior and leadership. I engage with a broad spectrum of clients, from individuals to larger teams and organizations, offering guidance in leadership development.

For a deeper dive into my professional background and consulting philosophy, several websites are available. There, you'll also find my contact details. I'm eager to hear your thoughts on the book or discuss potential collaboration in leadership coaching.

Discover more about my work and other publications related to leadership and organizational behavior at my personal website, https://thomaspatrickhuber.com.

Learn about my specific approach to leadership coaching and consulting at https://elevateus.ch, the official website of my company.

Lastly, in case you want to reach out to me directly please send me an email at thomaspatrick@mac.com.

I appreciate your support in purchasing this book and look forward to connecting with you.

Wishing you an enlightening journey,

Thomas P Huber, PhD, MS ECS

Dedication

This book is dedicated to the relentless seekers of growth—those who believe that leadership is not a title, but a continuous journey of learning, adaptation, and influence. To the mentors who light the path and the protégés who walk it with courage; to every executive who dares to look inward, challenging themselves to lead with empathy, integrity, and vision. May this guide serve as your compass, helping you navigate the complexities of leadership with grace and resilience, and may it inspire you to unlock not just your potential, but that of every individual whose life you touch. Here's to shaping the future, one leader at a time.

Foreword

Let's embark on a mission to illuminate the complexities and nuances of executive leadership coaching in today's rapidly changing world. This book represents not just a culmination of years of experience, research, and practice but also a deep-seated belief in the transformative power of leadership and coaching.

Leadership, in its essence, is a journey—one filled with challenges, learning, and growth. It requires a blend of strategic insight, emotional intelligence, and the ability to inspire and motivate others. Recognizing the solitude of this journey and the myriad obstacles leaders face, I aimed to create a comprehensive guide that would serve not only as a source of knowledge but as a companion through the intricacies of executive leadership development.

What differentiates this guide is its holistic approach to leadership coaching. It goes beyond traditional methodologies to delve into the psychological and emotional aspects that underpin effective leadership. The book underscores the importance of self-awareness, resilience, and personal branding, providing readers with a framework to not only enhance their coaching practices but also to foster their leadership capabilities.

The inclusion of practical exercises was a deliberate choice to ensure that the insights and strategies discussed could be applied and experienced firsthand. My intention was to encourage readers to engage actively with the content, fostering a deeper understanding and facilitating immediate application in their professional contexts.

Having navigated the challenges and rewards of leadership personally, I understand the transformative impact of a supportive and insightful coach. Through this book, I aspire to extend that support to you, the reader, whether you are an aspiring executive coach, a seasoned leader, or someone committed to personal and professional growth.

"Mastering Executive Leadership" is an invitation to join a community of leaders and coaches dedicated to excellence. As you turn these pages, I encourage you to see this not just as an opportunity to acquire new knowledge but as a call to action to apply these principles and exercises in your leadership journey.

Thank you for embarking on this journey with me. Together, let's inspire change, cultivate leadership, and unlock the potential within ourselves and others.

Sincerely,

Thomas P Huber, PhD, MS ECS

Lugano, 2024

Preface

The genesis of "Mastering Executive Leadership: A Coach's Guide to Unlocking Potential" lies in a simple yet profound realization: in our rapidly evolving global landscape, the demand for visionary and effective leaders has never been greater. As organizations grapple with unprecedented challenges and opportunities, the role of the executive coach becomes increasingly pivotal in shaping the leaders who will navigate these complexities with agility, insight, and integrity. This book is born out of a deep-seated desire to equip executive coaches, leaders, and all those passionate about leadership development with the insights, strategies, and tools necessary to foster outstanding leadership in themselves and others.

My journey into the realms of leadership and coaching has been both enriching and humbling. Over the years, I have had the privilege of working with a diverse array of leaders and aspiring coaches, each encounter enriching my understanding of the multifaceted nature of leadership. These experiences have underscored the importance of continuous learning, self-reflection, and the courage to face and embrace change. They have also highlighted the profound impact that a dedicated, insightful coach can have on an individual's path to leadership excellence.

This book synthesizes these learnings, drawing upon contemporary research, psychological insights, and practical experiences to offer a comprehensive guide to executive leadership coaching. It is designed to be both a reference and a workbook, blending theoretical frameworks with practical exercises that encourage active engagement and application of concepts.

The structure of this book mirrors the journey of leadership development, beginning with foundational concepts before moving into advanced strategies and coaching techniques. It is my hope that this progression will not only enhance your understanding of what effective leadership entails but also provide you with the tools to implement this knowledge in real-world contexts.

Writing this book has been a journey of discovery, filled with challenges, learnings, and moments of profound insight. My aim is to share these insights with you, to spark reflection, inspire action, and contribute to the ongoing dialogue on leadership and coaching. Whether you are an experienced coach, an emerging leader, or simply someone intrigued by the art and science of leadership, "Mastering Executive Leadership" is intended to be a valuable resource on your path to excellence.

As we step into the pages that follow, I invite you to approach this book not just as a reader, but as an active participant in your leadership development journey. The road to mastering executive leadership is ongoing, paved with challenges, but also abundant with opportunities for growth and transformation. Together, let's embark on this journey, equipped with the knowledge, skills, and determination to unlock the full potential of those we lead and coach.

Welcome to "Mastering Executive Leadership."

Introduction to Executive Leadership Coaching

In today's rapidly evolving business landscape, the demands on executive leaders are more challenging and complex than ever before. Globalization, technological advancements, and shifting societal expectations have transformed the way organizations operate, requiring leaders to adapt, innovate, and inspire like never before. It is within this dynamic context that executive leadership coaching emerges as an essential tool for developing the agile, strategic, and emotionally intelligent leaders that modern organizations need to thrive.

Executive leadership coaching is not merely a process but a transformative journey that empowers leaders to unlock their full potential, both personally and professionally. This journey is about more than just skill enhancement; it's about fostering a deep sense of self-awareness, cultivating resilience, and honing the ability to lead with vision and empathy. The role of an executive coach is to guide this journey, providing support, insight, and challenge to help leaders navigate the complexities of their roles and make a profound impact on their organizations and communities.

The purpose of this book is to offer a comprehensive exploration of executive leadership coaching, from its foundational principles and practices to the advanced techniques that can drive transformation and innovation. Whether you are an aspiring or seasoned executive coach, a leader seeking to enhance your effectiveness, or simply someone with a passion for personal and professional development, this book is designed to provide you with a wealth of knowledge, strategies, and tools.

As we embark on this journey together, I invite you to approach this book not just as a reader, but as an active participant in your own development and the development of those you lead or coach. The path to mastering executive leadership coaching is both challenging and rewarding, filled with opportunities for growth, learning, and transformation. Let us begin this journey with an open mind, a willingness to learn, and a commitment to becoming the best leaders and coaches we can be.

Executive leadership coaching is a focused, personalized process that aims to enhance the leadership capabilities of individuals at the highest levels of organizations. It plays a critical role in today's business environment, where the pace of change is relentless, and the demands on leaders are increasingly complex. Through one-on-one sessions, executive coaches work with leaders to uncover their strengths, address challenges, and develop skills necessary for effective leadership, such as strategic thinking, emotional intelligence, and decision-making.

This coaching process is not just about solving immediate problems but about fostering a deeper understanding of oneself and the dynamics of leading within a complex, global business landscape. It helps leaders to not only achieve their current objectives more effectively but also prepares them for future challenges by instilling in them the principles of adaptability, continuous learning, and visionary thinking.

The significance of executive leadership coaching lies in its ability to drive organizational success. Effective leaders inspire and motivate their teams, drive change and innovation, and create a culture of performance and engagement. In doing so, they significantly impact the organization's ability to compete and succeed in the modern business environment. Thus, executive leadership coaching is not just an investment in individual leaders but in the future of the entire organization.

Leadership, as a concept and practice, has undergone significant transformation over the centuries, evolving in tandem with the economic, social, and technological shifts that have shaped the business world. Historically, leadership in organizations was characterized by hierarchical, command-and-control models where power was centralized, and decision-making was top-down. This model was effective in the industrial age, where efficiency and standardization were the primary goals.

As we moved into the latter half of the 20th century and beyond, the business landscape began to change dramatically. The rise of the knowledge economy, the acceleration of technological innovation, and the increasing complexity of global markets demanded a new approach to leadership. The hierarchical models gave way to more flexible, collaborative forms of leadership, where the ability to adapt, innovate, and inspire became paramount.

The dawn of the 21st century has seen an even more pronounced shift towards leadership styles that prioritize emotional intelligence, inclusivity, and adaptability. This evolution reflects a broader understanding that leadership is not just about making strategic decisions or meeting financial targets; it's about creating a culture where employees feel valued, understood, and motivated to contribute their best work. Emotional intelligence, the capacity to be aware of, control, and express one's emotions, and to handle interpersonal relationships judiciously and empathetically, has emerged as a crucial leadership skill. Leaders who possess high emotional intelligence can better navigate the complexities of team dynamics, foster a positive work environment, and lead through change with sensitivity and resilience.

Inclusivity has also become a critical aspect of modern leadership. Today's leaders are expected to cultivate an environment that celebrates diversity, equity, and inclusion. By leveraging diverse perspectives and fostering a sense of belonging, leaders can drive innovation, improve problem-solving, and enhance organizational performance.

The rapid pace of change in today's business environment requires leaders to be exceptionally adaptive. They must be able to pivot quickly in response to market changes, technological advancements, and evolving customer needs. This agility enables organizations to remain competitive and relevant in a fast-moving world.

The evolution of leadership in the business world has been profound, moving from rigid, hierarchical models to more adaptive, emotionally intelligent, and inclusive approaches. This shift reflects a deeper understanding of the complex, dynamic nature of modern organizations and the central role that effective leadership plays in driving success. As we continue to navigate the challenges and opportunities of the 21st century, the ability of leaders to adapt, connect, and inspire will remain critical to their effectiveness and the prosperity of their organizations.

Leadership development is fundamental to both individual success and the overall performance of organizations. It represents a strategic investment in cultivating the skills and capabilities leaders need to navigate the complexities of the modern business environment effectively. This section explores why leadership development is crucial, its impact on various organizational facets, and the evidence supporting the value of investing in leadership initiatives.

Leadership development programs equip individuals with a broad range of competencies, including strategic thinking, emotional intelligence, decision-making, and the ability to lead through change. These competencies are essential for leaders at all levels to perform effectively in their roles, drive strategic initiatives, and achieve business objectives. For organizations, investing in leadership development means building a robust pipeline of capable leaders who can sustain growth, drive innovation, and navigate the challenges of an ever-changing business landscape. Effective leadership significantly influences organizational culture, setting the tone for the values, norms, and behaviors that define the workplace. Leaders who are committed to their own development and embody the principles of transparency, empathy, and integrity foster a positive culture that encourages collaboration, accountability, and mutual respect. Such a culture not only attracts and retains top talent but also enhances employee engagement and satisfaction, leading to higher productivity and performance.

Innovation is critical for organizational survival and success in the competitive 21st-century marketplace. Leadership development fosters an environment where creativity and innovation can flourish. Leaders equipped with skills in creative thinking, problem-solving, and risk-taking are better positioned to encourage a culture of innovation within their teams. They can inspire and empower employees to challenge the status quo, explore new ideas, and contribute to the organization's innovative efforts. The ability to withstand and recover from setbacks is another hallmark of successful organizations. Leadership development plays a vital role in building organizational resilience by preparing leaders to manage crises effectively, adapt to changes, and lead recovery efforts. Resilient leaders can maintain composure under pressure, make informed decisions in the face of uncertainty, and inspire confidence and hope among their teams, which is crucial for navigating through turbulent times.

Numerous studies and research findings underscore the value of leadership development. For instance, the Corporate Leadership Council's "Realizing the Full Potential of Rising Talent" report highlights a strong correlation between leadership development practices and critical business outcomes, including profitability and market share. Additionally, a study by the Center for Creative Leadership found that organizations with comprehensive leadership development programs outperformed their peers, reporting higher revenue growth, profitability, market share, and efficiency.

These findings make a compelling case for the strategic importance of leadership development. By investing in the growth and development of leaders, organizations not only enhance the capabilities of their current leadership team but also ensure a strong foundation for future success. Leadership development is not just an individual endeavor but a strategic imperative that shapes the destiny of organizations, making it crucial for sustainable growth, innovation, and resilience in an ever-evolving business environment.

Executive leadership coaching is a personalized, one-on-one process designed to enhance the leadership capabilities and effectiveness of individuals in high-level organizational roles. Unlike other forms of leadership development, such as workshops, seminars, or training programs, which often take a one-size-fits-all approach, executive coaching is highly customized to meet the specific needs, challenges, and goals of each leader. This bespoke process involves a partnership between the executive (coachee) and a professionally trained coach, focusing on targeted outcomes that benefit both the individual and the organization.

Leaders at the highest levels of organizations face a set of unique challenges that executive coaching is particularly well-suited to address. These include navigating complex organizational dynamics, making high-stakes decisions under conditions of uncertainty, managing stress and work-life balance, and leading change initiatives. Executive coaching provides a confidential and supportive space for leaders to explore these challenges, gain new perspectives, and develop strategies to overcome them. The personalized nature of coaching allows for deep dives into the specific issues that executives face, enabling tailored solutions that are not typically achievable through other leadership development methods.

The benefits of executive leadership coaching are extensive and impact both the individuals who undergo coaching and the organizations they lead. Some of the key benefits include:

- Enhanced Decision-Making: Executive coaching helps leaders improve their decision-making skills by fostering critical thinking, enhancing problem-solving capabilities, and reducing biases. Coaches encourage executives to consider multiple perspectives and potential outcomes, leading to more informed and strategic decisions.

- Increased Emotional Intelligence: Emotional intelligence (EQ) is crucial for effective leadership. Through coaching, executives can increase their self-awareness, manage their emotions more effectively, and develop greater empathy. This leads to better interpersonal relationships, improved team dynamics, and a more positive organizational culture.

- Improved Leadership Skills: Executive coaching focuses on developing a wide range of leadership skills, including communication, delegation, conflict resolution, and motivational techniques. Coaches work with executives to identify areas for improvement and develop actionable strategies to enhance these skills, leading to more effective leadership practices.

- Adaptability and Resilience: In today's fast-paced business environment, the ability to adapt to change and bounce back from setbacks is vital. Executive coaching helps leaders build resilience and flexibility, enabling them to navigate challenges and lead their organizations through periods of change with confidence.
- Personal and Professional Growth: Beyond specific leadership skills, executive coaching facilitates deep personal growth, helping leaders to align their personal values with their professional goals, enhance their work-life balance, and achieve greater job satisfaction and fulfillment.

Executive leadership coaching plays a pivotal role in developing the capabilities of top organizational leaders. By providing personalized support and targeted development, coaching addresses the unique challenges faced by executives and delivers a range of benefits that enhance individual performance, leadership effectiveness, and organizational success.

This book sets forth on an ambitious journey to provide a comprehensive guide for those on the path to becoming impactful executive coaches, as well as leaders aiming to elevate their own leadership prowess. At its core, it endeavors to equip its readers with a deep well of knowledge, encompassing the nuanced strategies, essential tools, and insightful principles necessary to navigate the multifaceted landscape of executive leadership in today's fast-paced business world. By delving into both the foundational and advanced aspects of coaching, the book is meticulously crafted to foster a profound understanding of the transformative capabilities inherent within effective leadership and the coaching processes that support it.

A key objective of this guide is to illuminate the pathway towards effective executive coaching, a discipline that demands a sophisticated blend of skills, from developing emotional intelligence and strategic thinking to mastering the art of motivation and change management. The book presents an array of coaching methodologies, underscored by real-world applications and theoretical underpinnings, to prepare coaches for the challenges they will face. It also focuses on enhancing leadership skills, offering leaders insights into harnessing their potential for driving innovation, leading with empathy, and making impactful decisions. Through this dual approach, the book aims to contribute significantly to the elevation of leadership quality across various organizational landscapes.

The intended audience for this book is as diverse as the subject matter it covers. It speaks directly to current and aspiring executive coaches, seeking to refine their craft and expand their coaching repertoire. Organizational leaders, from executives to middle managers, will find valuable insights into enhancing their leadership style and effectiveness. Human resources professionals and those involved in talent development and leadership training will also benefit from the comprehensive exploration of coaching strategies and leadership development principles presented herein. Additionally, anyone with a vested interest in the dynamics of leadership excellence and the transformative power of coaching will find this book to be an invaluable resource.

The book not only addresses the "how-tos" of executive coaching and leadership development but also delves into the "whys," exploring the underlying principles that make coaching an effective tool for leadership transformation. It examines the psychological aspects of leadership, the importance of emotional intelligence, and the impact of leadership styles on organizational culture and performance. By weaving together theory and practice, the guide aims to provide a holistic view of executive coaching, empowering readers to foster environments where leaders can thrive and drive meaningful change.

This book stands as a testament to the belief that effective leadership and skilled coaching are pivotal to organizational success and personal fulfillment. It aspires to serve as a beacon for those dedicated to the art and science of leadership, offering a path forward in the pursuit of excellence in executive coaching and leadership development. Whether you are at the beginning of your coaching journey, looking to enhance your leadership skills, or aiming to develop the leaders of tomorrow, this book is designed to support you every step of the way, offering insights, strategies, and inspiration to achieve your goals.

The structure of this book is thoughtfully designed to guide readers through the intricate journey of executive leadership coaching, unfolding across several distinct but interconnected parts. The initial sections lay the foundational knowledge necessary for understanding executive leadership and the principles of effective coaching. This includes an exploration of the evolution of leadership, the importance of leadership development, and the specific role that executive coaching plays within this context. By establishing a solid base, these sections ensure that readers grasp the critical concepts and challenges that shape the landscape of executive leadership today.

Following the foundational overview, the book transitions into more specialized topics, delving into advanced coaching techniques, the psychological underpinnings of leadership, and strategies for addressing common challenges faced by executives. These sections are designed to build upon the initial concepts introduced, offering deeper insights into the dynamics of leadership behavior, emotional intelligence, and the practical application of coaching strategies. Through real-world examples, case studies, and theoretical discussions, these parts of the book equip readers with the tools and understanding needed to navigate the complexities of executive coaching effectively.

An essential component of the book focuses on the practical application of coaching strategies in various contexts, including global leadership, cultural diversity, and leading through change. This section is particularly aimed at bridging the gap between theory and practice, providing readers with actionable frameworks, exercises, and techniques that can be applied directly to their coaching practice or leadership role. It's here that the book's objective to not only inform but also empower and inspire readers to apply their knowledge in real-world scenarios comes to fruition, emphasizing the transformative potential of effective coaching and leadership development.

The concluding sections of the book bring together the insights, strategies, and lessons learned, reiterating the book's core objectives and encouraging readers to continue their journey of growth and development. Appendices offering recommended readings, tools, templates, and resources for further exploration serve to reinforce the book's comprehensive approach to executive leadership coaching. By structuring the book in this way, each part contributes to a holistic understanding of what it means to be an effective coach and leader, ensuring that readers are well-equipped to inspire change, foster innovation, and lead with confidence in the modern business world.

This book is enriched with a variety of interactive components designed to deepen the reader's understanding and application of executive leadership coaching principles. These elements, including exercises, self-assessments, and reflection prompts, are carefully integrated throughout the book to transform passive reading into an active learning and self-discovery process. The inclusion of these components serves not only to reinforce the theoretical knowledge presented but also to enable readers to reflect on their personal leadership styles, identify areas for growth, and develop actionable strategies for improvement.

Exercises within the book are crafted to challenge readers to apply concepts in practical, real-world scenarios, simulating the complexities and nuances of executive leadership and coaching. These exercises range from role-playing situations that mirror common leadership challenges to strategic problem-solving tasks that require innovative thinking. By engaging with these exercises, readers can practice the skills and techniques discussed, gaining valuable insights into their effectiveness and areas for further development.

Self-assessments are another key interactive component, offering readers the opportunity to evaluate their competencies, emotional intelligence, leadership styles, and more. These assessments provide a structured framework for self-reflection, helping readers to gain a deeper understanding of their strengths and weaknesses. The insights garnered from these assessments are instrumental in guiding personal development plans and coaching strategies.

Reflection prompts scattered throughout the book encourage readers to pause and consider how the concepts discussed relate to their experiences, beliefs, and aspirations. These prompts are designed to foster a deeper level of introspection and connection with the material, encouraging readers to consider how they can integrate these learnings into their leadership and coaching practices.

Readers are strongly encouraged to actively engage with these interactive components, as doing so will significantly enhance their learning experience. By participating in exercises, completing self-assessments, and responding to reflection prompts, readers can transform theoretical knowledge into practical skills and insights. This active engagement is crucial for those looking to develop as effective leaders and executive coaches, as it not only solidifies understanding but also promotes continuous personal and professional growth. As you journey through this book, embrace these opportunities for engagement as stepping stones towards mastering the art and science of executive leadership coaching.

As you embark on this journey through the pages of this book, I invite you to approach it with an open mind and a genuine willingness to engage deeply with the material presented. The path to mastering executive leadership coaching is both challenging and profoundly rewarding, offering opportunities for personal and professional transformation that extend far beyond the confines of traditional leadership development.

The field of executive leadership coaching is dynamic and ever-evolving, reflecting the complexities of the modern business world. It demands not just the acquisition of new knowledge and skills but also a readiness to question existing beliefs and practices. By embracing the insights and strategies shared in this book, you have the opportunity to expand your understanding of what it means to lead and coach effectively in today's diverse and fast-paced environment.

The transformative potential of executive leadership coaching cannot be overstated. For coaches, it offers a chance to refine your craft, deepen your impact, and contribute to the development of leaders who are not only successful in achieving their objectives but also committed to fostering environments of inclusivity, innovation, and resilience. For leaders, engaging with the principles of coaching opens the door to unprecedented growth, enhancing your ability to inspire and motivate your teams, navigate complex challenges, and lead with vision and empathy.

This transformation begins with you—your willingness to introspect, to apply the concepts to your own experiences, and to embrace the continuous journey of learning and development. The exercises, self-assessments, and reflection prompts included in this book are designed to facilitate this process, encouraging you to not only understand the material intellectually but also to embody it in your daily practices as a coach or leader.

I encourage you to see this book not just as a source of information but as a catalyst for change. Allow yourself to be challenged, inspired, and ultimately transformed by the journey ahead. The field of executive leadership coaching offers boundless opportunities for those brave enough to explore its depths. As you move forward, remember that the greatest leaders and coaches are those who remain committed to their own growth and the empowerment of those they serve. Embrace this journey with curiosity, courage, and an open heart, and discover the profound impact you can make in the world of executive leadership.

The journey of leadership development is an essential pursuit in today's complex and rapidly changing business environment. The unique value that executive coaching brings to this endeavor cannot be overstated—it is a powerful tool for unlocking the potential of leaders, enabling them to navigate challenges with greater insight, adaptability, and resilience. Through the personalized and reflective nature of coaching, leaders can achieve not only professional growth but also personal transformation, leading to more effective leadership and, ultimately, more successful organizations.

As we stand at the threshold of this exploration into executive leadership coaching, it is important to recognize the profound impact that dedicated coaching can have on individuals and the teams and organizations they lead. This book aims to serve as your guide and companion on this journey, offering a blend of theory, practical strategies, and interactive components designed to deepen your understanding and enhance your practice.

I encourage you to embark on this journey with enthusiasm and dedication. The path to mastering executive leadership coaching is rich with opportunities for learning and growth. By engaging with the material presented, reflecting on your experiences, and applying the strategies and insights gained, you can contribute to the development of effective, inspirational leaders who are equipped to face the challenges of the 21st century.

Let this book inspire you to pursue excellence in your role as a coach or leader. Embrace the opportunity to make a significant impact in the lives of those you coach and lead, and in the broader landscape of your organization and community. The journey of mastering executive leadership coaching is one of discovery, challenge, and ultimately, transformation. Step forward with an open heart and a committed spirit, ready to explore the depths of leadership and coaching, and to realize the incredible potential that lies within.

Part I: Foundations of Executive Leadership Coaching

In the journey toward mastering executive leadership coaching, understanding the foundational elements that underpin effective leadership and coaching practices is paramount. Part I of this book, "Foundations of Executive Leadership Coaching," is designed to lay the groundwork for this understanding, providing readers with the essential knowledge needed to navigate the complexities of executive leadership in today's dynamic business environment.

The journey begins with a deep dive into the essence of executive leadership. We explore the definitions and key concepts that delineate what it means to lead at the executive level. Leadership is not just about holding a position of power; it's about influencing others, making strategic decisions, and setting a vision for the organization. The role of an executive leader has evolved significantly, necessitating a blend of strategic foresight, emotional intelligence, and the ability to drive transformational change.

We also confront the challenges that executive leaders face. From navigating organizational complexities to managing stakeholder expectations and fostering a culture of innovation, the landscape of executive leadership is fraught with challenges that require a nuanced approach to overcome.

Through self-reflection prompts and the identification of personal leadership examples, readers will engage in a process of introspection, evaluating their leadership qualities and identifying areas for growth.

Moving forward, we differentiate coaching from mentoring, elucidating the unique value that coaching brings to leadership development. Coaching is a personalized, goal-oriented approach that empowers leaders to unlock their potential and achieve specific outcomes. We outline the core principles of effective coaching, emphasizing the importance of active listening, powerful questioning, and fostering a coaching mindset.

The impact of coaching on executive development cannot be overstated. Through targeted interventions and support, coaching can catalyze profound personal and professional growth, enhancing a leader's ability to lead with confidence and clarity. By participating in role-playing coaching scenarios and drafting a personal coaching philosophy statement, readers will apply the principles discussed, gaining practical insights into the coaching process.

We explore the psychological underpinnings of effective leadership. Emotional intelligence, decision-making, and stress management are critical competencies for any leader, especially at the executive level. This section explores how leaders can harness their emotional intelligence to foster strong relationships and make informed decisions. We also discuss strategies for managing stress and building resilience, essential skills in the high-stakes environment of executive leadership.

Through emotional intelligence self-assessments and the creation of stress management plans, readers will develop strategies to enhance their psychological resilience, preparing them for the challenges of executive leadership.

Part I sets the stage for a comprehensive exploration of executive leadership coaching. By understanding the foundational elements of leadership, the essence of coaching, and the psychological aspects critical to leadership success, readers will be well-equipped to embark on the transformative journey of executive leadership coaching.

Chapter 1: Understanding Executive Leadership

In the intricate tapestry of modern organizations, understanding the nuances of executive leadership is more than a mere asset—it's a necessity. As the business landscape continues to evolve at an unprecedented pace, marked by rapid technological advancements, globalization, and shifting workforce dynamics, the role of executive leaders becomes increasingly complex and critical. These leaders are tasked not only with steering their organizations towards success but also with inspiring innovation, fostering a positive culture, and navigating the multifaceted challenges that arise in an ever-changing environment.

This section of the book is dedicated to unraveling the foundational concepts, roles, and challenges inherent in executive leadership. It aims to provide readers with a comprehensive understanding of what it means to lead at the executive level, highlighting the skills, qualities, and mindset necessary to excel in these high-stakes positions. By delving into the core aspects of executive leadership, this section sets the stage for a deeper exploration of how effective leadership can be developed and enhanced through coaching.

The purpose of this exploration is twofold: first, to equip current and aspiring executive leaders with the insights and tools they need to thrive in their roles, and second, to offer executive coaches a solid foundation upon which to build their coaching strategies. As we navigate through the intricacies of executive leadership, we'll examine the unique challenges faced by leaders in today's business world, from managing organizational change to leading diverse and geographically dispersed teams.

Understanding executive leadership within the context of modern organizations is not just about mastering a set of skills—it's about adopting a leadership approach that is adaptive, empathetic, and visionary. This section invites readers to engage with the material critically and reflectively, encouraging a journey of growth that extends beyond the pages of this book. Whether you are an executive leader seeking to enhance your impact or a coach dedicated to developing leadership excellence, this exploration serves as a foundational step in your journey towards mastering the art of executive leadership.

Leadership, in its broadest sense, encompasses the ability to guide, inspire, and influence others towards achieving common goals. It is an essential quality across various contexts, from small teams to entire organizations, and it involves a combination of skills, behaviors, and attitudes that facilitate effective direction and support to those being led. General leadership principles include vision setting, effective communication, decision-making, emotional intelligence, and the ability to motivate and empower others. These principles are universal, serving as the foundation for successful leadership in any capacity.

Executive leadership, while building upon these general principles, operates at a distinct level of complexity and responsibility. It refers specifically to the roles and practices of individuals in the highest tiers of organizational leadership, such as CEOs, presidents, and other C-suite executives. Executive leaders are responsible not only for setting the strategic direction of the organization but also for embodying its values, cultivating its culture, and ensuring its overall success and sustainability.

What differentiates executive leadership from other leadership roles is the scope of influence and the level of decision-making authority involved. Executive leaders must navigate a broader array of external and internal challenges, including global market dynamics, organizational change, and stakeholder management. They are also tasked with aligning various parts of the organization towards a cohesive strategy, often requiring a balance of strategic foresight, operational expertise, and interpersonal acumen.

Executive leadership demands a high degree of self-awareness and self-regulation, as executives set the tone for the entire organization. Their actions and decisions have a significant impact not only on the organization's direction but also on its culture and ethical standards. Thus, executive leaders must exhibit a profound understanding of their own leadership style and its effect on the organization's performance and morale.

While general leadership principles form the foundation of all leadership roles, executive leadership is distinguished by its focus on strategic decision-making, organizational alignment, and cultural stewardship at the highest level. Understanding the nuances of executive leadership is crucial for those aspiring to these roles and for those coaching leaders to achieve excellence in their capacity to guide their organizations towards success.

At the heart of effective executive leadership lies the ability to craft and communicate a compelling vision that serves as a guiding star for the organization. This vision encapsulates not just the long-term goals and aspirations of the organization but also the values and principles that underpin its operations. Executive leaders play a pivotal role in translating this vision into a strategic direction that informs planning, decision-making, and resource allocation across all levels of the organization. The articulation of a clear, inspiring vision fosters alignment among team members, stakeholders, and customers, creating a shared sense of purpose and commitment to achieving common objectives. Moreover, a well-defined vision enables leaders to steer their organizations through periods of change and uncertainty, maintaining focus and momentum towards long-term goals.

Decision-making at the executive level is characterized by its high stakes, complexity, and the broad implications of the outcomes. Executives are often faced with decisions that involve significant investments, strategic pivots, and operational overhauls. The process requires not only analytical skills and business acumen but also an understanding of the organization's internal dynamics and external environment. Effective executive leaders employ a decision-making approach that is both data-informed and intuitive, balancing empirical evidence with experiential insights. They are adept at considering multiple perspectives, assessing risks and opportunities, and making timely decisions that propel the organization forward. Additionally, transparency and inclusivity in the decision-making process can enhance trust and buy-in from team members, ensuring smoother implementation and greater resilience in the face of challenges.

Executive leaders wield a unique blend of influence and authority, derived not just from their formal positions but also from their personal credibility, expertise, and relational skills. The authority of executive leaders enables them to make critical decisions, allocate resources, and set priorities for the organization. However, it is their influence—the ability to inspire, persuade, and mobilize others—that truly amplifies their effectiveness. Influential leaders leverage their authority ethically and responsibly, fostering a culture of empowerment, collaboration, and innovation. They understand the importance of building and maintaining strong relationships, both within and outside the organization, to advance its interests and achieve its objectives. By aligning their influence with the organization's vision and values, executive leaders inspire commitment and drive collective action towards shared goals.

Together, these key concepts form the cornerstone of successful executive leadership. Vision provides direction, decision-making steers the course, and influence ensures the journey is undertaken with the full commitment and collaboration of all involved. Mastery of these areas is essential for any executive leader seeking to make a lasting impact on their organization and its stakeholders.

In the modern organization, the role of an executive leader transcends traditional boundaries, embedding itself deeply into the strategic fabric that defines and drives the entity's success. A crucial aspect of this role involves the setting and communication of a strategic vision, coupled with the meticulous execution of strategies to turn this vision into reality.

Executive leaders are the architects of their organizations' futures. They craft a strategic vision that outlines the long-term objectives and the overarching direction the organization aims to pursue. This vision, rooted in the organization's core values and purpose, serves as a north star, guiding decision-making, inspiring employees, and providing a clear framework for what success looks like.

The communication of this vision is as critical as its creation. Executive leaders must articulate the vision in a way that resonates across all levels of the organization, ensuring that it is understood, embraced, and acted upon. This involves translating the broader vision into actionable goals that teams and individuals can align with their daily activities. Effective leaders use storytelling, transparency, and engagement strategies to foster a shared sense of purpose, motivating employees to contribute their best towards the collective objectives.

Beyond setting the vision, executive leaders must also spearhead the execution of strategies designed to achieve the organization's goals. This entails a thorough understanding of the organization's internal and external environments, enabling leaders to devise strategies that are both ambitious and achievable. Execution involves meticulous planning, resource allocation, and the setting of clear, measurable objectives that align with the strategic vision.

Crucially, executive leaders play a pivotal role in building a culture that supports strategic execution. They model the behaviors and attitudes they wish to see, such as resilience, adaptability, and a commitment to excellence. They also establish mechanisms for monitoring progress, encouraging innovation, and adapting strategies in response to feedback and changing circumstances. By fostering a culture of accountability and continuous improvement, executive leaders ensure that the organization remains agile and focused, capable of overcoming obstacles and capitalizing on opportunities.

The role of an executive leader in setting and communicating a strategic vision, coupled with the execution of strategies to achieve organizational goals, is fundamental to the modern organization's success. Through their vision, executive leaders inspire and align their teams, while their focus on execution ensures that the vision is transformed into tangible outcomes. This dual focus on vision and execution underscores the essential role of executive leadership in navigating the complexities of today's business environment, driving growth, and securing the organization's future.

Change management has become an indispensable skill in the toolkit of effective executive leaders, reflecting the rapid pace of change in the global business environment. The ability to drive and manage organizational change is crucial for sustaining competitive advantage, responding to emerging opportunities, and addressing challenges. Executive leaders are at the forefront of orchestrating these changes, guiding their organizations through transitions with strategic insight and decisive action.

Executive leaders bear the primary responsibility for initiating change, whether it's in response to external market pressures, technological advancements, or internal inefficiencies. Their role involves identifying the need for change, crafting a clear vision of the post-change future, and developing a strategic plan to achieve this vision. Leaders must also be adept at rallying support for the change, communicating its benefits, and addressing any resistance within the organization. This requires not only strategic foresight but also a deep understanding of the organization's culture, values, and the diverse perspectives of its stakeholders.

One of the key challenges executive leaders face in managing change is maintaining momentum and alignment throughout the transition process. This involves setting clear, achievable milestones, providing the resources and support needed to achieve them, and continuously monitoring progress. Leaders must also be flexible, ready to adapt their strategies in response to new information or unexpected obstacles.

Strategies for Leading Through Transitions and Uncertainties

- Communicating Effectively: Clear, consistent, and transparent communication is vital during periods of change. Executive leaders should articulate the reasons for the change, the benefits it will bring, and the impact it will have on various stakeholders. Effective communication helps to build trust, mitigate concerns, and foster a sense of shared purpose among employees.

- Empowering and Engaging Employees: Empowering employees to contribute to the change process can enhance their commitment to the transition and encourage innovation. This may involve creating cross-functional teams, soliciting feedback and ideas, and recognizing and rewarding contributions to the change effort.

- Building Resilience and Adaptability: Executive leaders can lead by example, demonstrating resilience in the face of challenges and adaptability when plans need to change. By promoting a culture that values learning from setbacks and viewing failures as opportunities for growth, leaders can help their organizations navigate transitions more effectively.

- Supporting Employees: Change can be unsettling, and leaders must be attentive to the human aspect of transitions. Providing support, whether through training, counseling, or regular check-ins, can help employees adjust to new roles, processes, or technologies, ensuring a smoother transition.

- Fostering a Culture of Continuous Improvement: Embedding a culture of continuous improvement and openness to change can prepare an organization for future transitions, making change management an ongoing practice rather than a one-time event.

The executive leader's role in driving and managing organizational change is multifaceted, requiring a blend of strategic planning, effective communication, and emotional intelligence. By employing these strategies, leaders can navigate their organizations through transitions and uncertainties, transforming challenges into opportunities for growth and innovation.

Engaging with both internal and external stakeholders is a critical aspect of executive leadership, pivotal to the success and sustainability of any organization. Stakeholders, ranging from employees and customers to investors and community partners, have a vested interest in the organization's performance and strategic direction. Understanding and managing these diverse interests require a nuanced approach to communication and relationship building, skills that are essential for executive leaders to master.

The importance of stakeholder engagement lies in its ability to foster trust, alignment, and collaboration. By actively involving stakeholders in dialogue and decision-making processes, leaders can gain valuable insights, anticipate concerns, and mitigate potential conflicts. This proactive engagement not only enhances the organization's reputation but also strengthens its strategic position by ensuring that decisions are informed by a broad spectrum of perspectives.

Effective stakeholder communication begins with transparency and openness. Executive leaders should strive to communicate clearly and consistently, sharing information about organizational goals, changes, and challenges in a timely manner. This openness helps to build trust and demonstrates respect for stakeholders' roles and contributions to the organization.

Relationship building with stakeholders involves more than just communication; it requires a genuine effort to understand their needs, expectations, and concerns. This can be achieved through regular meetings, surveys, and forums that provide opportunities for stakeholders to express their views. Listening attentively to feedback and showing a willingness to adapt or address issues is crucial for maintaining positive and productive relationships.

Executive leaders can leverage technology and social media platforms to enhance stakeholder engagement. These tools offer additional channels for communication, allowing organizations to reach a wider audience and engage in real-time dialogue. However, the use of such platforms should be strategic and aligned with the organization's overall communication and engagement objectives.

Stakeholder engagement is a strategic imperative for executive leaders, requiring sophisticated communication skills and a commitment to building strong, mutually beneficial relationships. By prioritizing stakeholder engagement, leaders can ensure that their organizations remain responsive, resilient, and aligned with the broader ecosystem in which they operate. This not only supports organizational success but also contributes to the creation of sustainable value for all stakeholders involved.

In today's global business environment, leaders face an unprecedented level of complexity that demands agility, strategic foresight, and resilience. This complexity arises from a multitude of factors, including rapid technological advancements, global market fluctuations, evolving regulatory landscapes, and the increasing interconnectedness of economies. Such challenges are further compounded by the growing expectations for businesses to address social and environmental issues, adding layers of ambiguity and uncertainty to decision-making processes.

Navigating this complexity requires a multi-faceted approach that transcends traditional leadership models. Leaders must cultivate a deep understanding of the global context in which they operate, recognizing the interplay between various economic, technological, and societal forces. This understanding enables them to anticipate potential impacts on their organization and to identify opportunities for innovation and growth amidst the chaos.

One effective strategy for dealing with complexity and ambiguity is to foster a culture of continuous learning and adaptability within the organization. By encouraging teams to remain curious, to question assumptions, and to experiment with new ideas, leaders can create an environment that is resilient to change and capable of evolving in response to external pressures. This involves not only investing in the development of employees' skills and knowledge but also creating systems and processes that support flexibility and rapid response to emerging challenges.

Another key strategy is to enhance collaboration both within the organization and with external partners. Complex problems often require diverse perspectives and expertise to solve, making it essential for leaders to break down silos and facilitate cross-functional teamwork. Building strong networks with suppliers, customers, and other stakeholders can also provide valuable insights and resources that can be leveraged to navigate complexity more effectively.

Leaders must hone their ability to make decisions under conditions of uncertainty. This involves balancing thorough analysis with the intuition gained from experience, being prepared to take calculated risks, and developing contingency plans to mitigate potential adverse impacts. Transparent communication about the decision-making process, the rationale behind decisions, and the potential risks involved can help to build trust and alignment among stakeholders, even when outcomes are uncertain.

Navigating the complexity of today's global business environment requires leaders to be more adaptive, collaborative, and resilient than ever before. By fostering a culture of continuous learning, enhancing collaboration, and developing sophisticated decision-making capabilities, leaders can guide their organizations through the maze of contemporary challenges, turning potential threats into opportunities for innovation and growth.

The impact of technological advancements on executive leadership is both profound and multifaceted, reshaping how leaders strategize, operate, and engage with their teams and stakeholders. As digital technologies continue to evolve at a rapid pace, they bring about significant changes in market dynamics, consumer behaviors, and the very nature of competition. For executive leaders, this digital transformation presents a dual challenge: staying ahead in a technology-driven marketplace while fostering an organizational culture that embraces innovation and agility.

Adapting leadership styles to navigate this digital landscape effectively is crucial. Leaders must become champions of change, demonstrating a willingness to explore new technologies and to question traditional business models. This involves a shift from a command-and-control leadership approach to one that is more collaborative and facilitative. By empowering teams to experiment with innovative solutions and by creating a safe environment for taking calculated risks, leaders can stimulate creativity and accelerate digital adoption within their organizations.

Fostering innovation and agility in the digital age also requires leaders to be continuously informed about emerging technologies and their potential applications. This knowledge enables leaders to make strategic investments in technology that can enhance operational efficiency, improve customer experiences, and open up new avenues for growth. Moreover, by staying abreast of technological trends, leaders can better anticipate disruptions and position their organizations to respond proactively.

Another aspect of adapting to technological advancements involves cultivating digital literacy across all levels of the organization. Executive leaders play a key role in driving this initiative, advocating for ongoing digital education and skill development. By ensuring that employees are equipped to leverage new technologies effectively, leaders can enhance the organization's overall digital capability and foster a culture that is adaptable and forward-looking.

The digital age demands a new approach to leadership communication. With the rise of social media and digital communication platforms, leaders have unprecedented opportunities to engage with employees, customers, and other stakeholders directly and transparently. By harnessing these tools, leaders can strengthen connections, build trust, and galvanize support for their vision and strategic initiatives.

Adapting to technological advancements requires executive leaders to evolve their leadership styles, embracing innovation, collaboration, and continuous learning. By doing so, they can lead their organizations with agility and resilience, navigating the challenges and opportunities of the digital age with confidence.

In the high-pressure environment of executive leadership, the challenge of managing personal well-being alongside professional responsibilities is increasingly significant. The demands of leading an organization often extend beyond the conventional workday, encroaching on personal time and leading to a blurring of the lines between work and life. This imbalance can result in stress, burnout, and a decline in both personal health and professional performance. Recognizing and addressing this challenge is essential for sustaining long-term effectiveness and fulfillment in both domains.

Achieving a healthy work-life balance requires deliberate strategies and a commitment to self-care. Here are some tips and strategies for executives looking to navigate this balance more effectively:

- Set Clear Boundaries: Establish clear boundaries between work and personal life. This might involve setting specific work hours, designating times when work-related communications are off-limits, and creating physical or psychological separation between the work environment and home life.

- Prioritize and Delegate: Effective prioritization and delegation are key to managing workload and reducing stress. Identify the tasks that require your direct attention and those that can be delegated to team members. Trusting your team to handle delegated tasks not only lightens your load but also empowers them and fosters their development.

- Leverage Technology Wisely: While technology can enhance efficiency, it can also contribute to the blurring of work-life boundaries. Use technology smartly by taking advantage of tools that streamline your workflow and setting limits on technology use outside of designated work times.

- Schedule Downtime: Actively schedule time for relaxation and activities that rejuvenate your mind and body. Whether it's pursuing a hobby, spending time with family and friends, or simply unplugging from digital devices, ensure that downtime is a non-negotiable part of your schedule.

- Practice Self-care: Regular exercise, a healthy diet, and sufficient sleep are foundational to maintaining your physical and mental well-being. Make self-care practices a priority, recognizing that your health is the bedrock upon which your personal and professional success is built.

- Seek Support: Don't hesitate to seek support when needed. This can come from a variety of sources, including family, friends, professional networks, or mental health professionals. Sharing your experiences and challenges with trusted individuals can provide relief, insights, and strategies for managing stress and workload.

- Reflect and Adjust: Regularly reflect on your work-life balance and be prepared to make adjustments as needed. What works at one stage of your career or life may not be effective in another, necessitating continual reassessment and adaptation.

For executives, achieving a healthy work-life balance is not a one-time task but an ongoing process of negotiation and adaptation. By implementing these strategies and remaining vigilant about their well-being, leaders can ensure that they thrive both professionally and personally, leading their organizations with energy, clarity, and resilience.

In this chapter, we've embarked on a comprehensive exploration of the multifaceted nature of executive leadership, delving into its foundational concepts, the pivotal roles executive leaders play within modern organizations, and the unique challenges they encounter. From setting and communicating a strategic vision to managing complex organizational changes and engaging with a diverse array of stakeholders, the scope of executive leadership is both broad and deeply impactful. We've also touched on the critical importance of navigating technological advancements and maintaining a healthy work-life balance, underscoring the human aspect of leadership that is often overshadowed by strategic and operational demands.

The insights presented in this chapter serve as a foundation for understanding the complex landscape of executive leadership. However, knowledge alone is not sufficient. I encourage you to actively apply these concepts and engage with the exercises provided, integrating them into your leadership practice. By doing so, you can transform theoretical understanding into practical wisdom, enhancing your effectiveness as a leader and making a tangible impact on your organization.

As we transition to the next section, we will dive deeper into the essence of coaching, a vital skill set for any executive leader looking to cultivate a high-performing, motivated, and resilient team. Coaching extends beyond mere management, requiring a nuanced understanding of individual and team dynamics, the ability to inspire and empower, and the skills to facilitate growth and development. This next section will equip you with the strategies and tools necessary to unlock the full potential of your team members, fostering an environment of continuous learning and improvement.

Prepare to build upon the foundational knowledge of executive leadership with a focused exploration into coaching techniques, principles, and practices. By embracing the role of a coach, you can amplify your impact as a leader, driving your organization to new heights of success and innovation. Let's continue this journey together, deepening our understanding of what it means to lead and coach effectively in today's ever-evolving business landscape.

Exercises for Chapter 1: Understanding Executive Leadership

Exercise 1: Self-reflection on Leadership Qualities and Challenges

Objective: To enhance self-awareness by reflecting on your inherent leadership qualities and challenges.

Reflect on Your Leadership Qualities: Think about feedback you've received and moments you've felt effective as a leader. List at least three qualities that define your leadership.

Recall instances where you faced difficulties as a leader. Note down at least three significant challenges and describe one situation for each challenge.

Exercise 2: Guided Questions for Reflection

Objective: To deepen understanding of your leadership strengths and areas for improvement.

Instructions: Answer the following questions in your journal or a document:

- What leadership qualities have positively impacted your team or organization?

- When have you felt most effective as a leader, and why?

- How do others describe your leadership style, and what feedback on strengths have you consistently received?

- What specific skills or competencies do you need to develop further to enhance your leadership?

Exercise 3: Prompts for Identifying Leadership Challenges

Objective: To analyze personal leadership challenges and your strategies for navigating them.

Instructions:

1. Resistance to Change: Describe a time you encountered resistance to a new idea. How did you overcome it?

2. Leading Through Uncertainty: Recall leading through change or uncertainty. What strategies kept your team focused?

3. Learning from Failure: Reflect on a project or decision that didn't go as planned. How did you address the setback, and what did you learn?

Exercise 4: Identifying Personal Leadership Examples

Objective: To recognize and document instances demonstrating your executive leadership qualities.

Instructions:

1. Document Leadership Instances: Reflect on your leadership journey and identify specific instances where you demonstrated key executive leadership qualities such as strategic thinking, decisiveness, empathy, and resilience.

2. Analyze Outcomes and Lessons: For each instance, detail the outcomes and lessons learned. How did your leadership impact the situation, and what growth did you experience as a result?

As you engage with these exercises, allow yourself to be open and honest in your reflections. These activities are designed not only to highlight your strengths but also to illuminate areas where targeted development can lead to significant growth. Embrace this opportunity for self-discovery and consider how you can apply the insights gained to become a more effective leader. Reflecting on both successes and challenges enriches your leadership perspective, empowering you to lead with greater confidence, empathy, and strategic acumen.

Chapter 2: The Essence of Executive Coaching

As we transition from the broad and dynamic landscape of executive leadership into the focused and transformative world of executive coaching, we embark on a journey that delves into the heart of what it means to truly develop and empower leaders. Executive coaching stands as a pivotal practice within the realm of leadership development, offering a tailored, one-on-one approach that seeks to unlock the full potential of leaders at the highest levels of organizations. This chapter, "The Essence of Executive Coaching," aims to unravel the intricate tapestry of coaching practices, principles, and outcomes that define successful leadership coaching engagements.

Executive coaching is a sophisticated interplay between art and science, requiring a deep understanding of human behavior, motivation, and organizational dynamics. It is a collaborative process that fosters a confidential and trusting relationship between the coach and the executive, providing a safe space for vulnerability, introspection, and growth. Through this partnership, leaders are encouraged to explore their leadership style, confront their limitations, and harness their strengths in a manner that propels them toward their personal and professional objectives.

At its core, executive coaching is about facilitating change. Whether it's enhancing leadership skills, navigating career transitions, or fostering a more effective leadership presence, the goal of coaching is to initiate a process of transformation that extends beyond the individual to positively impact teams and the entire organization. This chapter will explore the key components that make executive coaching an effective development tool, including the establishment of clear goals, the use of evidence-based coaching methodologies, and the importance of measurable outcomes.

We will delve into the qualities and competencies that define an effective executive coach, including the ability to ask powerful questions, listen actively, and provide feedback that challenges and supports the executive in equal measure. The role of the coach as a mirror, mentor, and motivator will be examined, highlighting how these dynamics contribute to the executive's journey of self-discovery and leadership enhancement.

As we navigate through "The Essence of Executive Coaching," we invite readers to engage with an open mind and a reflective attitude. Whether you are an aspiring coach, an executive seeking to elevate your leadership capabilities, or a professional interested in the power of coaching, this chapter offers insights and guidance on the transformative potential of executive coaching. By understanding the essence of this practice, you can better appreciate its value in cultivating leaders who are not only equipped to face the challenges of today but are also prepared to lead with vision, empathy, and resilience in the ever-evolving landscape of the future.

Executive coaching is a personalized, goal-oriented developmental process tailored specifically to senior executives or individuals in high-level leadership positions within an organization. It focuses on enhancing the coachee's leadership capacity, performance, and personal effectiveness within the corporate context. This specialized form of coaching is characterized by its one-on-one format, providing a confidential and supportive environment where executives can explore their challenges, refine their skills, and achieve specific professional objectives.

At its core, executive coaching is about fostering a transformative learning experience. Unlike traditional forms of professional development, it does not follow a predetermined curriculum or instructional approach. Instead, it is a highly individualized process that centers on the unique needs, goals, and circumstances of the executive, making it a dynamic and flexible tool for leadership development. The coach and executive work together to identify areas for growth, set actionable goals, and devise strategies to overcome obstacles, leveraging the executive's strengths to facilitate positive change and professional advancement.

The distinction between executive coaching and other developmental interventions like mentoring, training, and consulting is crucial to understand the unique value executive coaching brings. Unlike mentoring, which often involves guidance and advice from a more experienced individual within the same field, executive coaching does not necessarily rely on the coach having direct experience in the executive's industry. The coach's expertise lies in their ability to facilitate growth through effective questioning, active listening, and evidence-based coaching techniques, rather than providing direct advice or solutions.

Training programs, while valuable for skill acquisition and knowledge enhancement, typically take place in a group setting and cover content that applies broadly to all participants. In contrast, executive coaching is deeply personal and singularly focused on the individual's development, providing tailored support that addresses specific leadership challenges and opportunities.

Consulting services, on the other hand, are designed to solve business problems or improve organizational performance, with consultants offering expert advice and solutions based on best practices. While consulting focuses on organizational outcomes, executive coaching concentrates on the personal growth and development of the executive, which, in turn, can lead to improved organizational performance as a natural outcome of enhanced leadership effectiveness.

Executive coaching stands out as a distinct and powerful approach to leadership development, offering personalized, goal-oriented support that catalyzes significant professional growth and transformation. By emphasizing the unique needs and aspirations of the executive, coaching facilitates a journey of self-discovery, skill enhancement, and strategic thinking that is unparalleled in its potential to elevate both leaders and the organizations they serve.

The executive coaching process is underpinned by several fundamental elements that ensure its effectiveness and transformative potential. These components create the foundation upon which successful coaching relationships are built, facilitating meaningful progress and sustainable change for the executive. Understanding these key elements is crucial for both coaches and executives to maximize the benefits of the coaching engagement.

Confidentiality is paramount in executive coaching. It establishes a secure environment where executives feel safe to share their thoughts, challenges, and vulnerabilities without fear of judgment or repercussions. This assurance of privacy encourages open dialogue and fosters a deeper level of introspection and honesty. For coaching to be truly effective, the executive must trust that the conversations, insights, and plans discussed will remain strictly between the coach and themselves. This confidentiality is critical not only for building trust but also for ensuring that the executive can explore and address sensitive issues that may be impacting their performance and leadership.

Trust is the cornerstone of the executive coaching relationship. It goes beyond the assurance of confidentiality to encompass the belief in the coach's expertise, intentions, and commitment to the executive's development. Trust develops over time, cultivated through consistent, respectful, and empathetic interactions. A strong trust foundation enables the coach to challenge the executive in ways that provoke growth while ensuring the executive remains open and receptive to feedback and new perspectives. For the executive, trusting the coach means believing in the process, even when it requires stepping out of their comfort zone or confronting uncomfortable truths.

Executive coaching is distinguished by its emphasis on achieving actionable outcomes. Unlike more theoretical or abstract forms of professional development, coaching engagements are goal-oriented, aiming to produce tangible improvements in leadership effectiveness, decision-making, and organizational impact. This focus on outcomes requires setting clear, measurable objectives at the outset of the coaching relationship, with both coach and executive committed to pursuing specific, agreed-upon goals. Action plans, accountability mechanisms, and regular progress assessments are integral to this process, ensuring that the coaching engagement remains dynamic and results-driven.

Together, these elements—confidentiality, trust, and a focus on actionable outcomes—form the bedrock of the executive coaching process. They ensure that the coaching engagement is a safe, supportive, and productive journey toward enhanced leadership capability and performance. By adhering to these foundational principles, executive coaching can unlock an individual's potential to lead with greater confidence, insight, and impact, driving meaningful change within themselves and their organizations.

Effective executive coaching is grounded in a set of foundational principles that ensure the process is conducted with professionalism, respect, and a genuine commitment to the client's growth and well-being. These principles not only guide the coach's behavior and decision-making but also create a framework within which the executive feels supported and empowered to explore, learn, and develop. A detailed exploration of these principles highlights their importance in facilitating a successful coaching engagement.

Ethical integrity is paramount in executive coaching, dictating that coaches operate within a framework of moral and professional standards. This involves adhering to a code of ethics that emphasizes respect for the individual, commitment to doing no harm, and ensuring that all coaching practices are conducted with the highest levels of honesty and fairness. Ethical integrity also means maintaining professional boundaries, recognizing the limits of one's competence, and referring clients to other professionals when their needs fall outside the coach's expertise. By upholding these ethical standards, coaches ensure that the coaching relationship is built on a foundation of trust and respect, essential for effective coaching outcomes.

A client-centered focus places the executive's needs, goals, and aspirations at the heart of the coaching process. This principle requires coaches to adopt a holistic view of the client, considering not only their professional challenges and objectives but also the broader context of their personal values, life experiences, and aspirations. The coaching process becomes a collaborative partnership, with the coach serving as a facilitator of the client's self-discovery and development. This approach empowers executives to take ownership of their growth, encourages self-directed learning, and ensures that the coaching outcomes are aligned with their personal and professional objectives.

Confidentiality is a critical principle that underpins the executive coaching process, creating a safe and private space for clients to explore their thoughts, feelings, and experiences without fear of exposure or judgment. Coaches must ensure that all information shared by the client during coaching sessions is kept confidential, except in cases where there is a legal or ethical obligation to disclose it. This principle extends to notes, records, and any communication about the coaching engagement, reinforcing the trust that is vital for an open and honest coaching relationship.

Respecting the client's autonomy involves recognizing and supporting their right to make their own choices and to direct their own life and development. While coaches provide insights, feedback, and guidance, they also acknowledge the executive's freedom to accept or reject suggestions and to choose their path. This respect for autonomy fosters a sense of empowerment and self-responsibility in the client, encouraging them to take active steps towards their development and to make decisions that are in line with their values and goals.

These foundational principles of ethical integrity, client-centered focus, confidentiality, and respect for autonomy are essential for creating a positive, effective, and ethical coaching relationship. By adhering to these principles, executive coaches ensure that their practices not only facilitate meaningful growth and development but also uphold the dignity, respect, and well-being of their clients.

Building effective relationships is a cornerstone of successful executive coaching, involving nuanced techniques that foster trust, rapport, and open communication between the coach and the executive. The foundation of these relationships is built on understanding and respecting the unique perspectives and experiences of the executive, creating a collaborative environment conducive to growth and development.

Rapport building is the initial step in establishing a productive coaching relationship. This process begins with creating a connection based on mutual respect and genuine interest in the executive's goals, challenges, and aspirations. Techniques for rapport building include active listening, where the coach fully engages with what the executive is saying without judgment or interruption, and mirroring, subtly reflecting the executive's body language, tone, and pace of speech to create a sense of alignment and understanding. These techniques help to break down barriers and foster a comfortable environment where the executive feels valued and understood.

Empathy is another critical component of effective coaching relationships. It involves the coach's ability to understand and share the feelings of the executive, seeing the world from their perspective. This empathetic approach helps executives feel supported and validated, encouraging them to open up and share their thoughts and feelings more freely. An empathetic coach can navigate the emotional landscape of the coaching process, responding to the executive's needs with compassion and sensitivity, and facilitating deeper self-awareness and personal growth.

Effective communication strategies are also vital for maintaining a productive coaching relationship. This encompasses not only the words used but also the manner in which they are delivered. Clear, concise, and transparent communication helps to avoid misunderstandings and ensures that both the coach and the executive are aligned in their objectives and expectations. Additionally, providing constructive feedback in a way that is direct yet supportive is crucial for helping executives recognize areas for improvement without feeling criticized or defensive. This approach encourages a positive, forward-looking perspective, focusing on solutions and opportunities for development rather than dwelling on past mistakes.

Together, these techniques of rapport building, demonstrating empathy, and employing effective communication strategies form the bedrock of a successful coaching relationship. By prioritizing the establishment and maintenance of this connection, coaches can create a dynamic and supportive environment that encourages executives to explore their potential, tackle challenges with confidence, and achieve their professional and personal objectives.

Active listening and inquiry are pivotal skills in the executive coaching process, playing a crucial role in facilitating self-awareness and discovery among executives. These skills enable coaches to delve deeper into the executives' experiences, perspectives, and challenges, fostering an environment of growth and learning. This kind of listening goes beyond simply hearing the words spoken by the executive; it involves fully engaging with the content and emotion behind those words. This means giving the executive undivided attention, observing non-verbal cues, and demonstrating understanding through verbal and non-verbal feedback. Techniques such as paraphrasing what the executive has said or summarizing key points help to confirm understanding and show that the coach is fully present in the conversation. Active listening creates a space where executives feel heard and valued, encouraging them to open up and share more freely, which is essential for effective coaching.

Inquiry, or the art of asking insightful questions, complements active listening by prompting deeper reflection and exploration. Effective coaches use open-ended questions that encourage executives to think critically about their behaviors, beliefs, and assumptions. These questions often begin with "what," "how," or "why," inviting detailed responses rather than simple yes or no answers. For instance, asking, "What was your thought process behind that decision?" or "How did that experience align with your values?" prompts the executive to reflect on their actions and motivations, fostering greater self-awareness.

The skillful combination of active listening and inquiry allows coaches to uncover underlying issues that may be impacting the executive's performance or satisfaction. By facilitating a deeper understanding of themselves, executives can identify areas for improvement, recognize their strengths, and develop strategies for overcoming obstacles. This process of self-discovery is vital for personal and professional development, enabling executives to make more informed decisions, improve their leadership skills, and ultimately achieve their goals.

Active listening and inquiry demonstrate the coach's genuine interest and commitment to the executive's development. When executives feel supported in this way, they are more likely to engage fully in the coaching process, take risks, and implement changes. Thus, these skills are not merely techniques but foundational elements of the coaching relationship that drive meaningful progress and transformation.

Goal setting and action planning are critical phases in the executive coaching process, serving as the bridge between the executive's current state and their desired outcomes. This process requires a collaborative effort, where both the coach and the executive work together to identify goals that are not only ambitious but also realistic and attainable. The essence of this collaboration is to ensure that the goals are deeply aligned with the executive's values, professional aspirations, and the broader objectives of the organization.

The first step involves establishing clear, specific goals that provide direction for the coaching engagement. These goals should be SMART: Specific, Measurable, Achievable, Relevant, and Time-bound. Specificity ensures that goals are well-defined and understandable; measurability allows for tracking progress;

achievability ensures that goals are realistic; relevance ensures alignment with the executive's values and objectives; and time-bound ensures that there is a clear deadline for achievement.

Coaches play a pivotal role in facilitating this process, guiding executives to articulate their visions for success in concrete terms. This might involve probing deeper into the executive's aspirations, challenging them to think beyond their immediate perceptions of what is possible, and helping them to identify the underlying motivations behind their goals. Through active listening and insightful questioning, coaches can help executives refine their goals to ensure they are meaningful and motivating.

Once goals are set, the next step is to develop strategic action plans to achieve them. This involves breaking down each goal into smaller, manageable tasks or milestones, each with its own set of actions, resources needed, and timelines. Action plans should be flexible enough to accommodate changes and adaptable to unforeseen challenges.

Coaches assist executives in mapping out these steps, encouraging them to think strategically about the most effective ways to achieve their goals. This might involve identifying potential obstacles and brainstorming strategies to overcome them, leveraging strengths and resources, and determining accountability measures to keep the executive on track.

An essential component of action planning is regular review and adjustment. Coaches and executives should establish checkpoints to assess progress towards goals, celebrate achievements, and recalibrate actions as needed. This iterative process ensures that the executive remains engaged and motivated, and that the action plan evolves in response to the executive's growth and changing circumstances.

Accountability mechanisms, such as regular check-ins with the coach, progress reports, or feedback sessions, are vital to maintaining momentum and ensuring commitment to the action plan. Coaches can provide the necessary support and encouragement to keep the executive focused and resilient in the face of challenges, reinforcing the importance of persistence and consistency in achieving long-term goals.

Goal setting and action planning are foundational to the success of the executive coaching process. Through a collaborative approach, coaches and executives can create a roadmap that not only guides the executive towards their desired outcomes but also fosters a sense of ownership and empowerment. This structured yet flexible approach ensures that the executive can navigate the path to their goals with clarity, confidence, and strategic focus.

Constructive feedback and reflective practices are integral components of the executive coaching process, playing a critical role in promoting personal growth and professional development. These elements facilitate a deeper understanding of one's behaviors, actions, and their impact on others, enabling executives to make informed adjustments and foster continuous improvement in their leadership journey. Feedback is essential for raising awareness and initiating change. It provides executives with an external perspective on their performance, highlighting strengths and identifying areas for development. Effective feedback is specific, timely, and focused on behavior rather than the individual. It is delivered in a manner that is clear and direct, yet sensitive to the recipient's feelings, fostering an environment of trust and openness.

In the context of executive coaching, feedback is a two-way street. Coaches provide insights based on observations, assessments, and the executive's self-reported experiences, offering recommendations for enhancing leadership effectiveness. Simultaneously, executives are encouraged to seek feedback from peers, subordinates, and other stakeholders, broadening their understanding of their leadership impact. This multifaceted approach ensures a comprehensive view, enabling executives to address blind spots and leverage their strengths more effectively.

Reflective practices complement feedback by encouraging executives to introspect and evaluate their experiences, behaviors, and the outcomes of their actions. Reflection involves taking a step back from the immediacy of daily activities to consider the broader implications of one's leadership approach. This might include journaling, meditation, or structured debriefing sessions with a coach, where executives can ponder questions like: "What went well? What could have been done differently? What did I learn from this experience?"

Reflection enables executives to internalize feedback, integrating new insights into their self-concept and leadership style. It fosters a growth mindset, where challenges are seen as opportunities for learning rather than threats to competence. Through regular reflective practice, executives can develop greater self-awareness, adaptability, and resilience, essential qualities for navigating the complexities of modern leadership.

Integrating feedback and reflection into professional development requires a deliberate and ongoing commitment. Executives should establish regular intervals for receiving feedback and engaging in reflective practices, embedding these activities into their routine. Coaches can facilitate this process by setting expectations for reflection, guiding executives in developing reflective questions, and providing frameworks for interpreting and acting on feedback.

Documenting insights and action plans as a result of feedback and reflection can be incredibly valuable. This documentation serves as a tangible record of the executive's growth journey, enabling them to track progress over time and adjust their development plans as needed.

Constructive feedback and reflective practices are vital for fostering a continuous cycle of learning, growth, and development in executive leadership. By embracing these elements, executives can enhance their self-awareness, refine their leadership skills, and achieve greater alignment between their actions and their leadership aspirations. Coaches play a pivotal role in guiding executives through this process, providing the support and structure needed to translate insights into actionable change.

Executive coaching plays a pivotal role in enhancing key leadership skills, crucial for navigating the complexities of today's dynamic business environment. Through targeted, personalized interventions, coaching provides a powerful platform for developing and refining the capabilities that define effective leadership. Among these, strategic decision-making, emotional intelligence, and team leadership stand out as fundamental skills that are particularly nurtured through the executive coaching process.

Strategic decision-making involves the ability to make informed, forward-looking choices that align with an organization's long-term goals and objectives. Executive coaching enhances this skill by fostering a space for leaders to explore and refine their approach to problem-solving and decision-making. Coaches encourage executives to think critically, challenging assumptions and considering multiple perspectives before arriving at a decision. This process is supported by techniques such as scenario planning, risk assessment, and the exploration of potential outcomes, which together contribute to a more nuanced and strategic approach to decision-making. Moreover, coaching helps executives to become more adept at navigating uncertainty, improving their ability to make decisions even in the face of incomplete information or rapidly changing conditions.

Emotional intelligence (EQ) is the capacity to understand and manage one's own emotions, as well as to recognize and influence the emotions of others. Executive coaching directly contributes to the development of EQ by encouraging self-reflection and greater self-awareness. Coaches work with executives to identify their emotional triggers and patterns of emotional response, providing strategies for managing emotions effectively. This heightened self-awareness also extends to empathy, enabling leaders to better understand and connect with their team members, stakeholders, and customers. By improving emotional intelligence, executive coaching helps leaders to build stronger relationships, enhance team cohesion, and foster a positive organizational culture.

Effective team leadership is about more than just managing a group of individuals; it involves inspiring, motivating, and guiding a team towards achieving shared goals. Executive coaching strengthens this aspect of leadership by equipping leaders with the skills to communicate vision, set clear expectations, and delegate responsibilities effectively. Coaches also focus on developing the leader's ability to build trust, resolve conflicts, and create an environment where team members feel valued and empowered. Through coaching, leaders learn to recognize the unique strengths and potential of their team members, adopting a more inclusive and collaborative leadership style that leverages diversity for enhanced team performance.

Executive coaching offers a valuable pathway for the enhancement of critical leadership skills. By focusing on strategic decision-making, emotional intelligence, and team leadership, coaching not only elevates the individual capabilities of leaders but also has a profound impact on the effectiveness and success of their organizations. Through personalized support and development, executive coaching empowers leaders to navigate the challenges of their roles with confidence, fostering a leadership approach that is strategic, emotionally intelligent, and team-oriented.

Coaching plays a pivotal role in supporting executives as they navigate career transitions, expand their leadership roles, and undergo personal transformation. These periods of change, while offering opportunities for growth, can also present significant challenges. Coaching provides a structured framework and supportive partnership that enables executives to approach these transitions with confidence, clarity, and a strategic mindset.

Career transitions, whether moving into a new industry, taking on a higher-level position, or even facing unexpected job changes, can be daunting for executives. Coaching aids in these transitions by offering a space for reflection and planning. Coaches help executives assess their strengths, values, and career aspirations, aligning them with new opportunities. Through coaching, executives can develop a clear vision for their next career phase, identify skills gaps that need to be addressed, and formulate a plan to successfully navigate the transition. Coaches also support executives in managing the emotional aspects of career change, building resilience, and maintaining a positive outlook throughout the process.

As executives take on larger leadership roles, they encounter new responsibilities, broader scopes of influence, and increased complexity in their decision-making. Coaching supports executives in this expansion by focusing on leadership development, strategic thinking, and the enhancement of emotional intelligence. Coaches work with executives to refine their leadership style, ensuring it is effective and aligns with the larger organizational goals. Furthermore, coaching provides strategies for effective team management, stakeholder engagement, and navigating organizational politics, all of which are crucial for success in expanded roles. Through targeted development and feedback, coaching enables executives to step confidently into larger roles, equipped with the skills and mindset necessary for effective leadership.

Personal transformation is often a byproduct of professional growth and career advancement. Coaching supports this transformation by encouraging executives to engage in deep self-reflection. This process allows them to examine their beliefs, behaviors, and impact on others, fostering greater self-awareness. Coaches challenge executives to step out of their comfort zones, question their assumptions, and explore new ways of thinking and leading. This can lead to significant shifts in an executive's approach to leadership, communication, and problem-solving. Personal transformation through coaching not only enhances an executive's professional effectiveness but also contributes to greater personal fulfillment and well-being.

Coaching also aids in the development of a growth mindset, where challenges are viewed as opportunities for learning rather than obstacles. This mindset is essential for continuous personal and professional development, enabling executives to remain adaptable and resilient in the face of change. By focusing on goals, providing accountability, and offering unwavering support, coaches help executives turn personal transformation into a strategic advantage.

Coaching is an invaluable tool for executives facing career transitions, expanding leadership roles, and undergoing personal transformation. It offers a supportive and challenging environment where executives can explore their potential, overcome barriers, and achieve significant growth. Through coaching, executives are better prepared to navigate the complexities of their roles and lead with greater impact, ultimately contributing to their own success and the success of their organizations.

Improved leadership through coaching translates into tangible organizational benefits, significantly impacting productivity, team dynamics, and the overall culture of the organization. By investing in the development of leaders, organizations can initiate a positive ripple effect that enhances performance and fosters a more engaging and supportive work environment.

Leadership coaching focuses on enhancing decision-making skills, strategic thinking, and problem-solving abilities among leaders. As these individuals learn to navigate challenges more effectively and make informed decisions swiftly, the pace of workflow and operational efficiency within the organization improves. Leaders who have undergone coaching are better equipped to set clear goals, prioritize tasks, and delegate responsibilities appropriately, ensuring that resources are utilized optimally. This streamlined approach to management not only boosts individual productivity but also elevates the performance of the entire team, contributing to the organization's overall productivity.

One of the key focuses of executive coaching is the development of emotional intelligence, including empathy, self-awareness, and the ability to manage one's emotions and relationships. Leaders who develop these skills are more adept at creating a positive and inclusive team environment, where open communication, trust, and collaboration are valued. They become more effective at conflict resolution, navigating interpersonal issues within the team with sensitivity and fairness. As a result, team dynamics improve, with members feeling more connected, supported, and motivated. This enhanced team cohesion leads to better collaboration, creativity, and innovation, driving the team towards achieving shared goals more efficiently.

The influence of leaders on organizational culture cannot be overstated; they set the tone for the values, behaviors, and norms that define the workplace. Through coaching, leaders develop a deeper understanding of their impact on culture and learn strategies for embodying and promoting the organization's core values. This might include leading by example, recognizing and rewarding behaviors that align with the organization's values, and addressing any actions that undermine them. As leaders become more intentional about cultivating a positive culture, they contribute to an environment where employees feel valued, respected, and engaged. This cultural enhancement leads to higher employee satisfaction and retention, a stronger sense of purpose and belonging among staff, and an overall improvement in organizational performance.

Leaders who engage in coaching often develop a coaching mindset themselves, adopting a more developmental approach to managing their teams. This not only supports the continuous growth and development of employees but also fosters a culture of learning and adaptability within the organization. By encouraging ongoing professional development, innovation, and open feedback, the organization becomes more resilient and better equipped to navigate the challenges of the modern business landscape.

The benefits of improved leadership through coaching are both broad and significant, affecting various aspects of organizational life. From increasing productivity and improving team dynamics to enhancing the overall culture, the impact of leadership coaching extends far beyond the individual leaders who participate in the coaching process. It contributes to a more dynamic, engaged, and high-performing organization, poised for success in an ever-changing business environment.

Initiating and managing a successful coaching engagement involves a structured approach that encompasses setting clear objectives, employing effective assessment tools, defining session structures, and establishing mechanisms for measuring progress. Here are the steps to ensure a coaching engagement is productive and impactful:

1. Establishing the Coaching Agreement

- Define Objectives: Begin by clarifying the goals of the coaching engagement with the executive. These should be aligned with both the individual's aspirations and the organization's strategic objectives.

- Set Expectations: Discuss and agree upon the expectations for both the coach and the executive, including confidentiality, commitment level, and the scope of the coaching relationship.

- Outline the Framework: Determine the duration of the coaching engagement, frequency of sessions, and any specific milestones or checkpoints.

2. Employing Assessment Tools

- Initial Assessments: Use a variety of tools to assess the executive's current leadership competencies, emotional intelligence, and other relevant areas. Tools may include 360-degree feedback, personality assessments, and strength finders.

- Identify Areas for Development: Analyze assessment results to identify strengths and areas for improvement. This analysis will guide the focus of the coaching sessions.

3. Defining Session Structures

- Setting the Agenda: Each coaching session should have a clear agenda, set collaboratively by the coach and the executive. The agenda should align with the overall coaching objectives and allow flexibility for emergent topics.

- Incorporating Variety: Employ a mix of discussion, reflection, exercises, and action planning to cater to different learning styles and keep the engagement dynamic.

- Ensuring Action Orientation: End each session with the development of actionable steps that the executive can take to apply learnings and move towards their goals.

4. Establishing a Feedback Loop

- Regular Check-ins: Incorporate regular check-ins within sessions to discuss progress, address any challenges, and adjust actions as necessary.

- Mid-point Review: Conduct a formal review at the midpoint of the engagement to assess progress towards goals, revisit initial assessments, and refine the focus for remaining sessions if needed.

5. Measuring Progress

- Define Success Metrics: At the outset, define clear metrics for success based on the coaching objectives. These could be related to specific leadership competencies, performance improvements, or feedback from peers and subordinates.
- Use Reflection and Assessment: Encourage ongoing reflection and utilize post-engagement assessments to measure progress against the initial benchmarks.

- Gather Feedback: Obtain feedback from the executive and relevant stakeholders to evaluate the impact of the coaching on the executive's leadership effectiveness and contribution to organizational goals.

6. Concluding the Engagement

- Review Achievements: Summarize the progress made towards the initial goals, highlighting key learnings and achievements.

- Plan for Continued Development: Develop a plan for how the executive can continue their development beyond the coaching engagement, including potential resources, follow-up sessions, or next steps in their leadership journey.

- Evaluate the Coaching Process: Reflect on the coaching process itself, gathering insights on what was most effective and areas for improvement in future engagements.

By following these steps, coaches can structure a coaching engagement that is tailored to the executive's needs, grounded in real-world challenges, and oriented towards achieving tangible improvements in leadership effectiveness and organizational impact.

Both coaches and clients may encounter a range of challenges that can hinder the progress of the coaching engagement. Recognizing these challenges early and addressing them with practical solutions is crucial to ensuring the coaching process is effective and delivers the desired outcomes.
One common challenge is establishing trust and rapport between the coach and the executive. Trust is the foundation of any coaching relationship, but it can take time to build, especially if the executive is skeptical about the coaching process or hesitant to open up. To overcome this, coaches should focus on creating a safe, confidential environment right from the start, emphasizing the non-judgmental nature of coaching and demonstrating empathy and understanding. Active listening and consistent follow-through on commitments can also help in building trust quickly.

Another challenge often faced during coaching engagements is resistance to change. Executives, like anyone, can be set in their ways and may struggle to step out of their comfort zones. This resistance can manifest as skepticism towards the coaching process or reluctance to implement new behaviors. Coaches can address this by helping executives to explore the underlying fears or beliefs that may be driving their resistance. Setting small, achievable goals can also encourage executives to take the first steps towards change, building momentum as they start to see positive results.

Lack of clarity regarding goals is another obstacle that can arise. Without clear, well-defined goals, coaching sessions may lack direction, making it difficult to measure progress. To combat this, coaches should work collaboratively with executives at the outset to identify specific, measurable, achievable, relevant, and time-bound (SMART) goals. Regularly revisiting and refining these goals can help keep the coaching engagement on track and ensure it remains aligned with the executive's evolving needs and aspirations.

Time constraints and scheduling conflicts are practical challenges that can impact the continuity and momentum of the coaching process. Busy executives may find it difficult to prioritize coaching sessions amidst their other responsibilities. To mitigate this, coaches and executives should agree on a regular schedule that works for both parties and commit to making coaching sessions a priority. Leveraging technology to facilitate remote sessions can also offer greater flexibility, making it easier to maintain consistent engagement.

Measuring the impact of coaching can be challenging, as improvements in leadership effectiveness are often qualitative and can take time to manifest. To address this, coaches should establish clear metrics for success at the beginning of the engagement and use a combination of qualitative and quantitative measures to assess progress. Soliciting feedback from peers, subordinates, and other stakeholders can also provide valuable insights into the executive's development and the broader impact of coaching on the organization.

By anticipating these challenges and implementing practical solutions, coaches can navigate the complexities of executive coaching engagements more effectively, fostering a productive and transformative experience for the executive and contributing to the achievement of their personal and professional goals.

Ensuring that the improvements gained through executive coaching are sustained over time and measuring the impact of coaching on both the executive and the organization, require strategic planning and ongoing evaluation. A holistic approach that integrates continuous learning, support systems, and feedback mechanisms can significantly enhance the durability of coaching outcomes and facilitate the measurement of its impact.

Sustaining improvements involves embedding the learned behaviors and strategies into the executive's daily routines. One effective strategy is the development of a long-term action plan that outlines specific practices the executive can continue to engage in post-coaching. This plan might include self-reflection exercises, continued learning opportunities such as workshops or courses, and structured peer mentoring or networking groups to provide ongoing support and encouragement.

Creating a culture of accountability within the organization further supports the sustainability of improvements. This can be achieved by setting up regular check-ins or follow-up sessions with the coach to review progress, discuss challenges, and recalibrate goals as necessary. Additionally, involving direct reports, peers, and superiors in the executive's development journey can foster an environment of mutual support and encouragement, reinforcing the changes and facilitating their integration into the organizational culture.

Measuring the impact of coaching on the executive and the organization involves both qualitative and quantitative methods. On an individual level, pre- and post-coaching assessments can be used to gauge changes in leadership competencies, emotional intelligence, and other relevant metrics. These assessments can be complemented by self-evaluations and feedback from colleagues to provide a comprehensive view of the executive's growth.

At the organizational level, key performance indicators (KPIs) related to team productivity, employee engagement, and organizational culture can offer insights into the broader effects of the coaching engagement. Increases in team performance, improvements in employee satisfaction surveys, and enhanced organizational agility may all be indicative of the positive impact of coaching. Additionally, tracking specific business outcomes related to the executive's goals, such as revenue growth, project completion rates, or customer satisfaction scores, can provide tangible evidence of coaching effectiveness.

Continuous feedback loops, where insights and observations from the measurement process are regularly reviewed and discussed, enable both the executive and the organization to make informed adjustments to strategies and practices. This ongoing evaluation not only highlights the value of the coaching investment but also ensures that the benefits are maximized and sustained over time.

Ensuring the sustainability of coaching improvements and measuring its impact require a comprehensive and integrated approach. By fostering a culture of continuous development and accountability and employing a mix of evaluative tools and feedback mechanisms, organizations can effectively sustain and assess the lasting benefits of executive coaching.

In concluding this exploration of executive coaching, we've delved deeply into its critical role in leadership development and organizational success. Executive coaching emerges not just as a tool for enhancing individual leadership capabilities but as a strategic asset that can significantly impact the broader dynamics of organizational performance and culture. Through the personalized, focused nature of the coaching relationship, executives are empowered to unlock their potential, navigate challenges with greater resilience, and lead with a renewed sense of purpose and vision.

The significance of executive coaching extends beyond the immediate benefits to the coached executives. It fosters a culture of continuous learning and improvement, encourages open communication and feedback, and enhances the overall leadership capacity within the organization. This ripple effect can lead to increased employee engagement, higher productivity, and a more agile and adaptable organizational structure, ultimately contributing to sustained success in an ever-changing business landscape.

As we reflect on the principles and strategies outlined in this chapter, it's clear that the practice of executive coaching is both an art and a science. Coaches are encouraged to apply these insights with flexibility and creativity, tailoring their approach to meet the unique needs and circumstances of each executive and organization. The strategies discussed—from building effective relationships and employing active listening and inquiry to setting goals and measuring progress—serve as a foundation upon which to build and refine your coaching practice.

The journey of becoming an effective executive coach is one of continuous learning and development. It demands a commitment to self-reflection, a willingness to embrace new perspectives, and an openness to feedback. The field of executive coaching is dynamic, evolving in response to new research, changing organizational needs, and the broader socio-economic environment. As such, coaches must remain lifelong learners, constantly seeking to enhance their skills, deepen their understanding of human behavior and organizational dynamics, and adapt their practices to remain effective and relevant.

In closing, this chapter underscores the transformative potential of executive coaching, both for individuals and organizations. By embracing the principles and strategies discussed, aspiring and seasoned coaches alike can contribute to the development of insightful, resilient, and effective leaders who are equipped to navigate the complexities of modern leadership. The journey is ongoing, filled with challenges and opportunities for growth. Yet, the rewards—witnessing the profound impact of your work on individuals and organizations—are immeasurable. As you continue to develop your practice, remember that the essence of executive coaching lies in the powerful partnership between coach and executive, a partnership that has the potential to change the course of careers, organizations, and indeed, lives.

Exercises for Chapter 2: Developing Coaching Skills

Exercise 5: Role-Playing Executive Coaching Scenarios

Objective: To enhance core coaching skills through the simulation of real-world coaching situations, enabling practitioners to practice and refine their approach in a controlled, reflective environment.

Instructions:

- Gather a Group: This exercise is most effective with a small group of fellow coaching practitioners, allowing for the roles of coach, executive, and observer to rotate among participants. If you're practicing alone, consider recording your role-play for self-review.

- Select Scenarios: Choose or create scenarios that reflect common coaching challenges, such as an executive struggling with delegation, conflict within a team, or navigating a career transition. Ensure scenarios are diverse to cover a broad spectrum of coaching issues.

- Assign Roles: In each role-play, assign one person to act as the coach, another as the executive, and others as observers. If in a pair, switch roles after each scenario to gain perspective from both sides.

- Conduct the Role-Play: Begin the exercise with the coach and executive engaging in a simulated coaching session based on the selected scenario. The coach should employ core coaching skills such as active listening, powerful questioning, and providing feedback. The session should aim to identify the executive's goal, explore the issue, and outline potential actions or solutions.

- Debrief: After each role-play, gather feedback from the observers, focusing on what the coach did well and areas for improvement. Discuss the coaching techniques that were most effective and why. The coach and executive should also reflect on their experiences, sharing insights into their feelings and reactions during the simulation.

- Reflect and Record: After the debrief, individually reflect on the exercise. What did you learn about your coaching style? What skills do you need to develop further? Record these reflections for future reference.

Exercise 6: Creating a Personal Coaching Development Plan

Objective: To create a structured plan for personal and professional development as an executive coach, focusing on identifying areas for growth and setting actionable steps to achieve coaching excellence.

Instructions:

- Self-Assessment: Begin with a thorough self-assessment of your coaching skills. Identify your strengths and areas for improvement, considering feedback you've received from coachees, peers, or mentors. Use coaching competencies frameworks as a guide.

- Define Growth Areas: Based on your assessment, select two to three key areas for growth. These might include developing deeper emotional intelligence, mastering specific coaching models, or enhancing your active listening and questioning skills.

- Set Learning Objectives: For each growth area, set specific, measurable learning objectives. What exactly do you want to achieve in this area, and how will you know when you've achieved it?
- Action Items: Develop a list of action items for each learning objective. This might include attending workshops or courses, reading specific books, seeking mentorship, or practicing new techniques in your coaching sessions.

- Timeline and Resources: Assign a realistic timeline to each action item and identify any resources you'll need, such as enrollment in courses, purchasing books, or scheduling time for practice and reflection.

- Accountability Mechanism: Determine how you will hold yourself accountable for achieving your development plan. This could involve regular check-ins with a mentor, joining a coaching study group, or setting up reminders to review your progress.

- Review and Adjust: Finally, plan for regular reviews of your development plan. As you grow and evolve as a coach, your areas for development and objectives may shift. Adjust your plan accordingly to ensure continuous growth and development.

By engaging in these exercises, coaches can actively work on refining their skills and approach, ensuring they are well-equipped to support their executives effectively and contribute to their success.

Chapter 3: Psychological Aspects of Executive Leadership

In the multifaceted realm of executive leadership, understanding the psychological dynamics at play is crucial for navigating the complex interactions and decisions that define the corporate landscape. This chapter delves into the significance of the psychological aspects of leadership within an executive context, highlighting how a leader's internal processes can profoundly influence their effectiveness, the well-being of their teams, and the overall success of the organization.

The psychological dimensions of leadership encompass a broad spectrum of factors, from emotional intelligence and cognitive styles to motivation, stress management, and resilience. These elements are not merely ancillary to the technical competencies required for executive roles; they are central to how leaders perceive challenges, engage with their teams, make decisions, and drive organizational change. Understanding these psychological underpinnings provides executives with a deeper insight into their leadership style, offering pathways to enhance their impact and foster a more dynamic, cohesive, and resilient organizational culture.

At the heart of these discussions is the concept of emotional intelligence—the capacity to be aware of, control, and express one's emotions, and to handle interpersonal relationships judiciously and empathetically. Emotional intelligence is a critical determinant of effective leadership, enabling executives to navigate the emotional complexities of the workplace, build stronger relationships, and create an environment of trust and collaboration.

Similarly, the exploration of decision-making processes unveils the cognitive and emotional factors that influence how choices are made, the biases that can skew judgment, and the strategies that can enhance decision quality. This understanding is pivotal for executives, who often face high-stakes decisions under conditions of uncertainty.

The chapter addresses how leaders can manage stress, maintain resilience in the face of challenges, and support their teams in doing the same. In today's fast-paced and often volatile business environment, the ability to cope with stress and bounce back from setbacks is invaluable for sustaining performance and well-being.

By examining the psychological aspects of executive leadership, this chapter aims to equip leaders with the insights and tools needed to refine their leadership approach, enhance their interpersonal dynamics, and lead with greater awareness, empathy, and strategic acumen. As we explore these psychological dimensions, executives are encouraged to reflect on their experiences and consider how integrating these insights can elevate their leadership and contribute to the flourishing of their organizations.

Understanding emotional intelligence (EI) is fundamental to grasping the nuances of effective leadership, especially within the high-stakes environment executives navigate. Emotional intelligence refers to the capacity of individuals to recognize, understand, and manage their own emotions and those of others. This multifaceted concept encompasses five critical components: self-awareness, self-regulation, motivation, empathy, and social skills. Each element plays a distinct role in shaping how leaders perceive and respond to the challenges and opportunities they encounter.

- Self-awareness is the foundation of EI, involving an understanding of one's emotions, strengths, weaknesses, and values, and how these impact others. It enables leaders to assess situations accurately and make informed decisions without being overly influenced by emotional undercurrents.

- Self-regulation refers to the ability to control or redirect disruptive emotions and impulses and to adapt to changing circumstances. Leaders who excel in self-regulation can maintain their composure under pressure, think before acting, and express their emotions in appropriate ways.

- Motivation in the context of EI is characterized by a passion to work for reasons that go beyond money or status and a propensity to pursue goals with energy and persistence. This intrinsic drive helps leaders stay focused on objectives, overcome obstacles, and inspire the same level of commitment from their teams.

- Empathy is the ability to understand the emotional makeup of other people and to treat them according to their emotional reactions. Empathetic leaders can build and maintain rapport with a diverse range of individuals, sense their team members' feelings and perspectives, and effectively address grievances, fostering a positive work environment.

- Social skills, the final component of EI, involve managing relationships to move people in the desired direction. Leaders with strong social skills are adept at communication, conflict resolution, and building networks. They know how to inspire and influence others, facilitating teamwork and collaboration towards common goals.

The importance of emotional intelligence in leadership effectiveness and organizational success cannot be overstated. Leaders with high EI are better equipped to handle the demands of their roles, from making complex decisions to navigating the intricacies of team dynamics. They create more cohesive and motivated teams, drive higher levels of employee engagement and satisfaction, and foster organizational cultures characterized by resilience and adaptability.

Emotional intelligence plays a crucial role in leadership development. By focusing on enhancing their EI, leaders can improve their capacity to deal with stress, adapt to change, and inspire others. This not only benefits their personal growth but also contributes significantly to the overall health and performance of the organization. In essence, the development of emotional intelligence among executives is not just an individual endeavor but a strategic investment in the future success and sustainability of the organization.

Developing emotional intelligence (EI) is a journey that requires commitment, self-reflection, and practice. By focusing on enhancing each component of EI, leaders can significantly improve their leadership effectiveness and their ability to drive organizational success. Here, we explore strategies for improving each aspect of EI, alongside real-world examples of how these qualities manifest in executive leadership.

Developing Self-awareness involves regularly reflecting on your emotions and the impact they have on your decisions and actions. Keeping a journal, seeking feedback from trusted colleagues, and practicing mindfulness can help you become more attuned to your internal states. A real-world example of self-awareness in action is an executive who recognizes their tendency to react defensively to criticism. By acknowledging this pattern, they can work on responding more constructively, fostering a culture of open communication and continuous improvement.

Enhancing Self-regulation can be achieved by identifying emotional triggers and developing strategies to manage them, such as taking a moment to breathe deeply or pause before responding to challenging situations. An executive who successfully self-regulates might encounter a stressful project setback and, instead of assigning blame or reacting impulsively, calmly assesses the situation to identify a solution, demonstrating control and resilience.

Boosting Motivation in oneself can be cultivated by setting personal and professional goals that are aligned with one's values and finding intrinsic rewards in the pursuit of these goals, beyond external recognition or compensation. For example, an executive motivated by a genuine desire to innovate might lead their team through a challenging product development process, maintaining enthusiasm and focus even in the face of obstacles, inspiring their team through their passion and dedication.

Improving Empathy requires actively listening to others, putting oneself in their shoes, and acknowledging their perspectives and feelings. An empathetic executive might notice a team member appearing disengaged and take the time to understand their concerns, providing support or adjustments as needed. This not only addresses the team member's needs but also strengthens trust and loyalty within the team.

Strengthening Social Skills involves practicing effective communication, conflict resolution, and relationship-building techniques. Joining networking groups, engaging in team-building activities, and seeking mentorship opportunities can enhance these skills. An example of strong social skills in executive leadership might be a leader who navigates a complex negotiation with stakeholders from different backgrounds, leveraging their ability to communicate clearly, build rapport, and find a mutually beneficial solution.

Each of these strategies contributes to the development of a well-rounded, emotionally intelligent leader capable of navigating the complexities of modern executive roles. Real-world examples of emotional intelligence in action highlight its transformative potential, not only in enhancing individual leadership performance but also in fostering a positive, productive organizational environment. Through continuous effort to develop EI, executives can lead more effectively, inspire their teams, and drive their organizations toward greater success.

Decision-making is a complex cognitive process that involves a delicate balance between intuitive and analytical thinking. Intuitive thinking, often referred to as 'gut feeling,' is fast, automatic, and emotion-driven. It is based on the experiences and knowledge that leaders accumulate over time, allowing them to make quick judgments in situations where speed is of the essence.

On the other hand, analytical thinking is slow, deliberate, and logical. It involves systematically processing information, weighing options, and considering potential outcomes to arrive at a reasoned decision.

Both intuitive and analytical thinking have their place in executive decision-making. Intuitive thinking is particularly useful in high-pressure situations where there is no time for detailed analysis, or when the decision at hand involves factors that are difficult to quantify. Analytical thinking, however, is invaluable for complex decisions that require thorough consideration of data and potential implications. Effective leaders are those who can seamlessly switch between these two modes of thinking, applying each where it is most appropriate.

The decision-making process is often influenced by common biases and heuristics that can lead to suboptimal outcomes. One such bias is confirmation bias, where individuals tend to favor information that confirms their preexisting beliefs or hypotheses, disregarding evidence that contradicts them. This can lead executives to make decisions based on incomplete or selective information, potentially overlooking critical risks or alternative solutions.

Another notable heuristic is the availability heuristic, where decisions are influenced by information that is most readily available, rather than all relevant information. This can result in an overemphasis on recent events or highly memorable experiences, skewing risk assessment and decision-making priorities.

The anchoring bias also plays a significant role in decision-making, particularly in negotiations or financial decisions. It refers to the tendency to rely too heavily on the first piece of information offered (the "anchor") when making decisions, which can lead to insufficient adjustment from that starting point.

Overcoming these biases requires a conscious effort to recognize their influence and actively counteract them. Strategies for mitigating biases include seeking out diverse perspectives, implementing structured decision-making processes that encourage critical evaluation of all available data, and using techniques such as pre-mortems, where potential failures in a decision are anticipated and analyzed before they occur.

Understanding the cognitive processes involved in decision-making, including the interplay between intuitive and analytical thinking, as well as recognizing and mitigating common biases and heuristics, is crucial for effective executive leadership. By developing an awareness of these dynamics, executives can enhance their decision-making capabilities, leading to better outcomes for themselves and their organizations.

Mitigating biases and improving the quality of decisions in the executive realm necessitate a multifaceted approach, blending critical thinking, emotional intelligence, and systematic strategies to counteract cognitive shortcuts and distortions.

- Diverse Perspectives: Actively seeking input from individuals with diverse backgrounds, expertise, and viewpoints can counteract narrow thinking and introduce new insights, challenging prevailing assumptions and uncovering blind spots.

- Structured Decision-making Processes: Implementing structured frameworks for decision-making, such as decision trees or cost-benefit analyses, encourages thorough evaluation of options and outcomes, reducing reliance on intuition or flawed heuristics.

- Reflection and Review: Building in time for reflection before finalizing decisions allows for a more measured approach, reducing the impact of emotional reactions or impulsive judgments. Regularly reviewing past decisions, both successes and failures, can also provide valuable learning opportunities, highlighting tendencies towards certain biases and revealing patterns that can be corrected in future decisions.

- Pre-commitment to Criteria: Establishing clear criteria for decision-making in advance can help maintain objectivity and focus on relevant factors, reducing the influence of irrelevant information or emotional sway.

Critical thinking is essential for effective decision-making, enabling leaders to analyze information logically, identify logical fallacies, and differentiate between strong and weak arguments. It involves questioning assumptions, evaluating the validity and reliability of data, and considering alternative viewpoints and solutions. By fostering a culture of critical thinking within their teams, executives can enhance collective decision-making capabilities, encouraging a more analytical and evidence-based approach to tackling challenges.

Emotional intelligence (EI) plays a complementary role, equipping leaders with the awareness and regulation skills necessary to manage the emotional dimensions of decision-making. High EI enables executives to recognize their emotional reactions and biases, understand their impact on judgment, and navigate the emotions of others effectively. This awareness can prevent emotions from clouding judgment, ensuring that decisions are made with a balance of empathy and logic. Additionally, EI fosters better communication and conflict resolution skills, which are crucial for building consensus and buy-in for decisions within the organization.

Integrating critical thinking and emotional intelligence into the decision-making process not only mitigates biases but also enriches the quality of decisions. Leaders who harness these skills can navigate complex situations with greater clarity, nuance, and effectiveness, leading to outcomes that are more aligned with organizational goals and values. As such, developing these capabilities should be a priority for executives seeking to enhance their leadership impact and drive their organizations toward sustained success.

Understanding stress in the context of leadership is crucial, as it significantly impacts executive performance and well-being.

Stress, in its essence, is the body's response to any demand or challenge. In the high-stakes, fast-paced environment of executive leadership, stress is an inevitable part of the job. However, not all stress is detrimental. It is essential to differentiate between positive stress, known as eustress, and negative stress, referred to as distress, to manage it effectively and harness its potential to enhance leadership capabilities.

Stress manifests through a combination of physical, emotional, and psychological responses when an individual perceives a discrepancy between the demands placed on them and their ability to meet those demands. These responses can include changes in physiology, emotions, and behavior, and they serve as a mechanism to cope with perceived threats or challenges. For executives, these demands often relate to organizational performance, decision-making, team leadership, and balancing professional and personal responsibilities.

The impact of stress on executive performance and well-being can be profound. In moderate amounts, stress (eustress) can act as a motivator, enhancing focus, energy, and productivity. It can drive executives to achieve goals, tackle new challenges, and step out of their comfort zones, contributing to personal growth and organizational success. Eustress is typically characterized by feelings of excitement, satisfaction, and accomplishment.

Conversely, excessive or prolonged stress (distress) can have detrimental effects. It can impair cognitive functions such as memory, attention, and decision-making, and lead to emotional symptoms like irritability, anxiety, and depression. Physically, distress can contribute to a range of health issues, including cardiovascular disease, sleep disturbances, and weakened immune function. In the long term, unmanaged distress can lead to burnout, significantly diminishing an executive's effectiveness and overall quality of life.

Differentiating between eustress and distress is key to managing stress effectively. Eustress is generally associated with positive experiences and outcomes. It is the type of stress experienced when taking on a manageable challenge, learning a new skill, or achieving a milestone. Eustress is motivating and energizing, often leading to a sense of fulfillment and increased resilience.

Distress, on the other hand, occurs when challenges become overwhelming, persistent, and seemingly insurmountable. It is marked by feelings of being out of control, overwhelmed, and unable to cope. The distinction between eustress and distress often lies in the individual's perception of their ability to manage the situation and the resources they have available to them.

Understanding and differentiating between these types of stress enable executives to identify when stress is becoming harmful and take proactive steps to mitigate its effects. Strategies may include delegating tasks, seeking support, implementing stress-reduction techniques, and ensuring a healthy work-life balance. By recognizing the signals of distress and addressing them early, executives can maintain their performance levels, protect their well-being, and continue to lead effectively amidst the pressures of their roles.

Building resilience is essential for executives to effectively handle stress, adversity, and the inevitable challenges that accompany leadership roles. Resilience refers to the ability to bounce back from setbacks, adapt to change, and continue to pursue one's goals with perseverance and determination. It's not just about surviving difficult situations but thriving amidst them. Developing resilience involves a combination of mindset, behaviors, and strategies that can be cultivated over time.

Here are some strategies for developing resilience:

- Foster a Growth Mindset: Embrace challenges as opportunities for learning and growth. Viewing setbacks not as insurmountable obstacles but as valuable feedback helps in developing a more resilient approach to problem-solving and decision-making.

- Build Strong Relationships: Supportive relationships are a cornerstone of resilience. Cultivating a network of trusted colleagues, mentors, and friends provides emotional support and practical advice during difficult times. These connections can offer new perspectives, encouragement, and a sense of belonging.

- Practice Self-care: Taking care of one's physical and mental health is crucial for resilience. Regular physical activity, adequate rest, healthy eating, and mindfulness practices like meditation can enhance your ability to cope with stress and recover from adversity.

- Set Realistic Goals and Take Action: Break down larger goals into manageable tasks and focus on taking small, actionable steps forward. This approach fosters a sense of accomplishment and progress, even in the face of challenges.

- Learn from Experience: Reflect on past experiences, both successes and failures, to identify lessons learned and strengths developed. This reflection can increase self-awareness and confidence in your ability to navigate future challenges.

- Maintain Perspective: Try to view stressful situations from a broader perspective and keep long-term goals in mind. This can help in assessing challenges more objectively and reducing the overwhelming nature of immediate problems.

In the context of leadership, resilience is not just a personal asset but a critical component of effective leadership. Leaders who demonstrate resilience inspire confidence in their teams, fostering a culture of perseverance and adaptability. This is especially important in times of uncertainty or significant organizational change, where the ability to navigate ambiguity and maintain a positive outlook can significantly influence team morale and performance.

Resilient leaders are also more capable of making reasoned, strategic decisions under pressure, as they can manage their emotions and focus on solutions rather than being paralyzed by the fear of failure. Moreover, by modeling resilience, leaders encourage their teams to develop these same qualities, enhancing the overall resilience of the organization.

Resilience equips leaders with the tools to handle stress and adversity more effectively, enabling them to lead their teams through challenges with confidence and poise. By developing resilience, leaders can ensure that they, and their organizations, are not just surviving but thriving, ready to seize opportunities and navigate the complexities of the modern business landscape.

Integrating emotional intelligence, decision-making strategies, and resilience into daily leadership practices is essential for executives aiming to enhance their effectiveness and maintain psychological well-being amidst their demanding roles. This holistic approach not only improves leadership performance but also contributes to a more positive and productive organizational culture.

Emotional intelligence underpins effective leadership by enabling executives to manage their emotions and understand those of others, fostering strong relationships and a supportive work environment. To integrate emotional intelligence into daily practices, executives should start by actively listening to their team members, showing empathy, and being open to feedback. This involves acknowledging different perspectives and addressing emotions in a constructive manner, which can enhance team cohesion and conflict resolution.

Incorporating decision-making strategies into daily leadership involves being mindful of the cognitive processes that influence choices and taking steps to ensure decisions are both rational and aligned with organizational goals. This can be achieved by pausing to reflect before making significant decisions, seeking diverse viewpoints to challenge assumptions, and employing structured decision-making frameworks to evaluate options systematically. Cultivating a practice of reflective decision-making helps in minimizing biases and encourages a more analytical approach to solving complex problems.

Building resilience is crucial for navigating the uncertainties and pressures inherent in executive roles. Daily practices that contribute to resilience include setting clear boundaries between work and personal life to prevent burnout, prioritizing tasks to focus on what is most important, and maintaining a positive outlook even in the face of setbacks. Encouraging a culture of openness and learning from mistakes within the team also strengthens collective resilience, enabling the organization to adapt and thrive in changing circumstances.

Maintaining psychological well-being while fulfilling executive responsibilities requires a conscious effort to manage stress and prioritize self-care. This involves recognizing the signs of excessive stress and taking proactive steps to address it, such as engaging in regular physical activity, practicing mindfulness or relaxation techniques, and ensuring adequate rest. Additionally, cultivating interests and relationships outside of work can provide a valuable counterbalance to the pressures of executive life, offering opportunities for relaxation and rejuvenation.

Seeking support when needed, whether through professional counseling, coaching, or peer networks, can provide executives with additional strategies for managing challenges and maintaining their psychological health. By integrating emotional intelligence, decision-making strategies, and resilience into their daily practices, and by prioritizing their well-being, executives can enhance their leadership effectiveness and contribute to a healthier, more resilient organizational culture.

In wrapping up our exploration of the psychological aspects of executive leadership, it's clear that the interplay between emotional intelligence, decision-making abilities, and resilience is foundational to navigating the multifaceted challenges of leadership roles. These psychological factors are not peripheral traits but central competencies that significantly influence an executive's capacity to lead effectively, inspire teams, and drive organizational success.

Leaders are encouraged to recognize the importance of ongoing development in these areas. Cultivating emotional intelligence not only enhances interpersonal relationships and team dynamics but also equips leaders to manage their emotions and those of others more effectively. Similarly, honing decision-making skills, grounded in both intuition and analysis, enables leaders to navigate uncertainty with confidence and clarity. Furthermore, building resilience is crucial for sustaining performance under pressure, adapting to change, and overcoming obstacles.

The journey towards enhancing these psychological competencies is continuous and demands a commitment to self-reflection and personal growth. Leaders should seek opportunities for learning and development, whether through formal training, coaching, or self-directed learning. Engaging in reflective practices, seeking feedback, and embracing challenges as opportunities for growth are all strategies that can support this developmental process.

Final thoughts emphasize the paramount importance of self-awareness and psychological well-being in sustaining not only leadership effectiveness but also personal fulfillment. Leaders who invest in understanding themselves and prioritizing their well-being set a powerful example for others and contribute to creating a positive organizational culture. In essence, the pursuit of psychological development in leadership is a pursuit of excellence, not just in professional capacities but in the quality of life and the impact leaders have on the world around them. By embracing the complexity and depth of psychological factors in leadership, executives can navigate their roles with greater insight, empathy, and resilience, leading to more meaningful and fulfilling leadership experiences.

Exercises for Chapter 3: Psychological Aspects of Executive Leadership

Exercise 7: Emotional Intelligence Self-Assessment

This guided self-assessment exercise is designed to help you evaluate your emotional intelligence (EI) levels across its five core components: self-awareness, self-regulation, motivation, empathy, and social skills. By reflecting on your experiences and behaviors, you can identify areas of strength and opportunities for growth in your EI.

Step 1: Rate Your EI Components

For each EI component, consider recent professional interactions and situations. Rate your perceived proficiency in each area on a scale from 1 (needs significant improvement) to 5 (excellent).

Step 2: Reflection Questions

- Self-awareness: Think of a recent situation where your emotions affected your behavior. How accurately were you able to identify and understand your emotions?

- Self-regulation: Recall a moment of stress or anger in the workplace. How did you manage your response?

- Motivation: Consider a challenging project or goal. What drove you to pursue it, and how did you maintain your enthusiasm?

- Empathy: Reflect on a time a colleague was experiencing difficulty. How did you respond, and what was the outcome?

- Social Skills: Think about a recent team project. How effectively did you communicate and manage relationships?

Step 3: Identifying Growth Opportunities

Based on your ratings and reflections, identify which EI components you excel in and which could use further development. Outline specific situations where enhancing your EI could have or would improve the outcome.

Step 4: Action Plan

Choose one area for improvement and set one actionable goal for development. This could involve seeking feedback, engaging in relevant training, or practicing specific EI strategies in your daily interactions.

Exercise 8: Stress Management Plan Creation

Creating a personalized stress management plan involves identifying strategies and practices that can help you effectively manage stress, promoting well-being and resilience. This plan will serve as a roadmap for incorporating these techniques into your routine.

Step 1: Identify Stressors

Reflect on your recent experiences to identify specific situations, tasks, or interactions that trigger stress. List these stressors and note any patterns or common themes.

Step 2: Choose Stress Management Techniques

For each identified stressor, choose a corresponding stress management technique. Techniques may include mindfulness meditation, time management strategies, physical activity, or engaging in hobbies. Consider a variety of approaches to address different aspects of stress.

Step 3: Develop Your Plan

Outline a weekly schedule that incorporates your chosen stress management techniques. Be realistic about what is achievable, considering your current commitments and lifestyle.

Step 4: Commit to Practice

Make a commitment to yourself to practice your stress management techniques regularly. Set reminders if helpful, and consider enlisting a colleague, friend, or family member for support and accountability.

Step 5: Monitor and Adjust

After implementing your plan for a few weeks, reflect on its effectiveness. Have your stress levels decreased? Do you feel more resilient? Adjust your plan based on what is working and what is not, experimenting with different techniques as needed.

Step 6: Reflect on Your Experience

Reflect on the process of creating and following your stress management plan. Consider how the practice of regular stress management has impacted your well-being and leadership effectiveness.

By engaging in these exercises, you take a proactive step toward enhancing your emotional intelligence and managing stress more effectively, laying the foundation for stronger leadership and a more fulfilling professional life.

Part II: Strategies for Effective Executive Coaching

As we progress in our exploration of executive leadership coaching, Part II, "Strategies for Effective Coaching," shifts our focus from foundational concepts to the practical strategies and techniques that enable coaches to facilitate meaningful development in leaders. This section is dedicated to equipping coaches with the tools and insights necessary to guide leaders through a transformative journey, enhancing their skills, and elevating their performance to new heights.

The cornerstone of any successful coaching engagement is a thorough assessment and clear goal setting. This chapter delves into the importance of identifying leadership strengths and areas for development as the first step in a coaching relationship. By understanding where a leader excels and where there is room for growth, coaches can tailor their approach to meet the specific needs of each leader.

Setting SMART goals—Specific, Measurable, Achievable, Relevant, and Time-bound—is essential for ensuring that leadership development efforts are focused and effective. We explore various tools and techniques for assessment, from 360-degree feedback to personality inventories, providing coaches with a repertoire of resources to facilitate insightful evaluations.

Readers will engage with leadership assessment tools provided in the book, applying these instruments to either themselves or fictional case studies. Additionally, the process of setting personal SMART goals will help readers practice goal-setting principles in a concrete way.

Leadership extends beyond strategic decision-making; it encompasses a range of interpersonal and cognitive skills critical for success. This chapter focuses on developing key leadership skills such as communication, strategic thinking, problem-solving, influencing, and negotiation. Each of these areas is vital for effective leadership, and enhancing these skills can significantly impact a leader's ability to guide their organization toward its goals.

Through practical advice and actionable strategies, coaches will learn how to support leaders in refining these skills, fostering a well-rounded leadership profile that can navigate the complexities of the business world with confidence.

The inclusion of exercises such as a communication style inventory and strategic challenge simulations allows readers to assess their communication preferences and apply strategic thinking to real-world problems, deepening their understanding and proficiency in these essential skills.

Performance enhancement goes beyond skill development, encompassing the optimization of a leader's workflow, feedback mechanisms, and their approach to learning. This chapter presents strategies for improving leader performance through effective feedback, time management techniques, and fostering a culture of continuous learning within their teams and organizations.

By implementing these strategies, leaders can enhance their productivity, adaptability, and resilience, ensuring they are well-equipped to meet the challenges and opportunities that lie ahead.

Practical exercises, such as conducting a feedback session with a peer and adopting a time management tool for a week, offer readers the opportunity to practice these strategies in real-life scenarios, reinforcing the learning experience.

Part II of "Mastering Executive Leadership" provides a comprehensive toolkit for coaches and leaders alike, offering strategies that address the multifaceted aspects of leadership development. Through assessment, skill development, and performance enhancement, this section lays the groundwork for achieving lasting change and exceptional leadership.

Chapter 4: Assessment and Goal Setting

In leadership development, the processes of assessment and goal setting are indispensable. They serve as the compass and roadmap, guiding leaders through the complex terrain of personal growth and organizational achievement. This chapter delves into the crucial roles these processes play in enhancing leadership capabilities, ensuring that development efforts are both strategic and aligned with overarching objectives.

The importance of assessment in leadership development cannot be overstated. A thorough and accurate assessment provides a clear snapshot of a leader's current competencies, pinpointing both strengths and areas in need of improvement. This evaluation is foundational, as it informs the subsequent steps in the development journey. By utilizing a variety of assessment tools, including 360-degree feedback, personality inventories, and performance reviews, leaders can gain a multifaceted understanding of their leadership style, impact, and effectiveness. Such insights are invaluable, not only for personal awareness and growth but also for understanding how leaders are perceived within their organizations.

Following assessment, goal setting emerges as the critical next step. It transforms the insights gained from assessment into actionable pathways for development. Effective goal setting in leadership development is characterized by specificity, relevance, and alignment with both personal aspirations and the strategic goals of the organization. This process ensures that development efforts are focused, measurable, and capable of producing tangible improvements in leadership performance.

Goal setting empowers leaders to take ownership of their development, encouraging a proactive approach to enhancing their skills and addressing gaps. By setting clear, achievable goals, leaders can chart a course for continuous improvement, leveraging their strengths and making strategic adjustments to overcome challenges. This alignment of individual development with organizational objectives also ensures that leadership growth contributes directly to the success and resilience of the organization as a whole.

The processes of assessment and goal setting are foundational to effective leadership development. They ensure that efforts to enhance leadership capabilities are informed, targeted, and aligned with the broader vision and needs of the organization. As we explore these processes further, we will uncover the strategies and best practices that can maximize their impact, enabling leaders to achieve their full potential and drive meaningful organizational change.

In the ever-evolving landscape of leadership development, various frameworks and models stand as pivotal tools for evaluating leadership competencies and behaviors. These frameworks serve not only as benchmarks for what effective leadership looks like but also provide a structured approach to identifying areas of strength and opportunities for growth. This introduction will explore some of these essential frameworks and models, highlighting their contributions to understanding and enhancing leadership effectiveness. Additionally, we'll delve into the benefits of self-awareness in leadership, underscoring its critical role in maximizing a leader's impact.

Leadership competency frameworks often categorize competencies into clusters such as strategic thinking, emotional intelligence, communication, team building, and decision-making, among others. Models like the Leadership Practices Inventory (LPI) focus on behaviors that are demonstrable and observable, suggesting that leadership is not just about traits but about actions that inspire, challenge, enable, model, and encourage others. Similarly, the Emotional Competency Inventory (ECI) provides insights into emotional intelligence competencies, emphasizing their importance in effective leadership.

Another influential model, Daniel Goleman's Six Leadership Styles, derived from emotional intelligence, posits that the most effective leaders are those who can flexibly switch between styles—such as authoritative, democratic, and coaching—depending on the situation. Meanwhile, the Situational Leadership Model emphasizes the adaptability of leadership styles to the development level of team members, advocating for a more personalized approach to leadership.

These frameworks and models offer valuable lenses through which leaders can assess and refine their approach, ensuring their leadership is both effective and responsive to the needs of their team and organization. They facilitate a structured self-evaluation, encouraging leaders to reflect on their practices and behaviors critically.

The benefits of self-awareness in this context are manifold. Self-aware leaders are better equipped to understand their impact on others, recognize their strengths and limitations, and identify how their leadership style influences team dynamics and organizational culture. This level of self-knowledge is crucial for personal growth, as it informs targeted development efforts and guides leaders in seeking feedback and learning opportunities.

Self-awareness enhances emotional intelligence, enabling leaders to manage their emotions and those of others more effectively, fostering a positive and productive work environment. It also supports adaptability, allowing leaders to adjust their approach in response to feedback, changing circumstances, or the evolving needs of their team.

The integration of established frameworks and models for evaluating leadership competencies, coupled with a commitment to self-awareness, lays the foundation for leadership effectiveness. These tools not only guide leaders in honing their skills but also underscore the importance of reflection and adaptability in achieving leadership excellence. As leaders embark on this journey of self-discovery and development, they unlock their potential to inspire, influence, and drive meaningful change within their organizations.

The role of feedback in leadership development is pivotal, providing a mirror through which leaders can view their performance, behaviors, and impact on others from multiple perspectives. 360-degree feedback, performance reviews, and informal feedback each play a unique part in this process, offering insights into leadership strengths and areas for development. Understanding how to effectively solicit and interpret this feedback is crucial for leaders seeking to enhance their effectiveness and drive personal growth.

360-Degree Feedback offers a comprehensive view of a leader's competencies and behaviors by gathering insights from a wide range of sources, including superiors, peers, subordinates, and sometimes even clients. This type of feedback is invaluable for its holistic perspective, shedding light on how a leader's actions are perceived across different levels of the organization. It highlights discrepancies between self-perception and the perception of others, uncovering blind spots and reaffirming strengths.

Performance Reviews are typically more formal assessments conducted by supervisors or HR departments. They focus on evaluating a leader's performance against predefined objectives and competencies. While they may not offer as broad a perspective as 360-degree feedback, performance reviews provide structured, objective assessments of a leader's contributions to organizational goals, offering a basis for identifying development priorities.

Informal Feedback occurs in day-to-day interactions and can be just as valuable as formal methods. It often provides real-time insights into a leader's impact, allowing for immediate reflection and adjustment. Informal feedback can come from casual conversations, direct observations, or spontaneous comments, offering a more dynamic and responsive gauge of leadership effectiveness.

Strategies for Soliciting and Interpreting Feedback Constructively Creating a Culture of Openness: Leaders can foster an environment where feedback is regularly exchanged and valued. This involves modeling receptiveness to feedback, encouraging open dialogue, and demonstrating appreciation for constructive input, regardless of its source.

- Asking Specific Questions: When soliciting feedback, it's beneficial to ask specific, targeted questions rather than general ones. This approach elicits more actionable insights. For example, asking, "How could I have handled the team meeting more effectively?" provides clearer guidance than a broad inquiry like, "How am I doing?"

- Seeking Diverse Perspectives: To avoid bias and gain a well-rounded understanding, leaders should seek feedback from a variety of sources. This diversity can highlight different aspects of leadership practice and reveal patterns or inconsistencies in behavior and impact.

- Reflecting and Analyzing Feedback: Upon receiving feedback, take time to reflect and analyze it critically. Consider the context in which the feedback was given and look for underlying themes. It's important to differentiate between feedback that reflects personal styles and preferences versus that which points to areas genuinely needing improvement.

- Developing an Action Plan: Based on feedback, identify specific areas for development and create an action plan. This plan should include measurable goals, strategies for improvement, and mechanisms for tracking progress. Revisit and adjust the plan as needed, based on ongoing feedback and self-assessment.

- Maintaining Emotional Balance: Receiving feedback, especially if critical, can be challenging. It's crucial to maintain emotional balance, viewing feedback as a valuable opportunity for growth rather than a personal attack.

Developing this perspective is integral to using feedback constructively.

Integrating feedback into leadership development is an ongoing process that requires commitment, openness, and resilience. By effectively soliciting and interpreting feedback, leaders can gain profound insights into their strengths and areas for growth, paving the way for continuous improvement and enhanced leadership effectiveness.

The principles of SMART goal setting provide a robust framework for leaders aiming to enhance their capabilities and effectiveness. SMART, an acronym for Specific, Measurable, Achievable, Relevant, and Time-bound, outlines criteria that can help ensure goals are clear and reachable within a specified timeframe. This structured approach is particularly beneficial in leadership development planning, where goals must be carefully designed to foster growth, accountability, and progress.

Principles of SMART Goal Setting

1. Specific: Goals should be clear and specific to avoid ambiguity. A specific goal should detail what needs to be accomplished, why it's important, who's involved, where it's located, and which resources or limits are involved. This clarity helps to focus efforts and clearly define what success looks like.

2. Measurable: Including precise amounts, dates, and other measurable indicators in your goals helps to track progress and stay motivated. Assessing progress helps leaders to stay focused, meet deadlines, and feel the excitement of getting closer to achieving their goal.

3. Achievable: While goals should be ambitious, they also need to be realistic and attainable to be successful. An achievable goal will usually answer questions such as: How can I accomplish this goal? How realistic is the goal, based on other constraints, such as financial factors?

4. Relevant: A goal must matter to you and align with other relevant goals. Essentially, it should be worthwhile and match other efforts and needs. A relevant goal can answer "yes" to these questions: Does this seem worthwhile? Is this the right time? Does this match our other efforts/needs?

5. Time-bound: Every goal needs a target date, so that you have a deadline to focus on and something to work toward. This part of the SMART goal criteria helps to prevent everyday tasks from taking priority over your longer-term goals.

Examples of SMART Goals Tailored to Leadership Development

Example 1: Enhance Emotional Intelligence

- Specific: Improve my emotional intelligence to enhance team communication and conflict resolution.

- Measurable: Increase emotional intelligence score by 10 points on the Emotional Intelligence Appraisal test.

- Achievable: Enroll in an emotional intelligence workshop and practice strategies daily.

- Relevant: Enhancing emotional intelligence will improve team dynamics and project outcomes.

- Time-bound: Achieve this goal within the next six months.

Example 2: Develop Strategic Thinking Skills

- Specific: Develop strategic thinking skills to contribute to the organization's long-term planning process.

- Measurable: Lead a strategic project that contributes to one of the organization's key strategic goals.

- Achievable: Attend a course on strategic thinking and apply techniques learned to daily decision-making.

- Relevant: Strategic thinking is essential for my role as it aligns with my career path and the needs of the organization.

- Time-bound: Complete the strategic thinking course in three months and lead a project in the following quarter.

Example 3: Improve Public Speaking Skills

- Specific: Enhance public speaking skills to effectively communicate company vision and project updates to stakeholders.

- Measurable: Deliver a presentation at the company-wide meeting with positive feedback from at least 75% of attendees.

- Achievable: Participate in a public speaking workshop and practice by presenting at smaller team meetings.

- Relevant: Being an effective communicator is crucial for leadership to inspire and inform the team and stakeholders.

- Time-bound: Accomplish this goal before the next annual company meeting in nine months.

Setting SMART goals in leadership development is a powerful way to achieve clarity, structure, and motivation. By applying these principles, leaders can outline a path for their growth that is both ambitious and attainable, ensuring that their development efforts lead to meaningful improvements in their leadership effectiveness.

Ensuring that leadership development goals are aligned with personal values and the strategic direction of the organization is crucial for the effectiveness and fulfillment of any leader. This alignment not only enhances the leader's motivation and engagement but also ensures that their growth contributes positively to the organization's success. Achieving this synergy involves a thoughtful process of reflection, communication, and integration of personal and organizational objectives.

The first step in aligning leadership development goals with personal values involves deep reflection. Leaders should take time to articulate their core values and consider how these values influence their leadership style, decision-making, and interactions with others. This self-awareness is foundational, as it guides leaders in choosing development goals that resonate with their beliefs and aspirations. When leadership development goals are rooted in personal values, leaders are more likely to pursue these goals with passion and persistence, leading to more significant personal and professional growth.

Equally important is a comprehensive understanding of the organization's vision, mission, and strategic objectives. Leaders should engage in regular dialogue with other executives and stakeholders to grasp the broader organizational goals and the context in which their leadership operates. This understanding allows leaders to identify areas where their personal growth can most effectively contribute to the organization's needs. For instance, if an organization is aiming to enhance its innovation capabilities, a leader might focus on developing skills in creative thinking and fostering a culture of innovation within their team.

Integrating personal values with the organization's strategic direction involves identifying the intersection between the two. Leaders should ask themselves how their unique strengths and values can address the current and future needs of the organization. This might involve setting goals to enhance communication skills, strategic planning abilities, or emotional intelligence, depending on both the leader's personal growth areas and the organization's priorities.

Leaders should seek feedback and support from mentors, coaches, or peers to refine their goals and strategies for achieving this alignment. Regularly revisiting and adjusting these goals ensures they remain relevant to both personal aspirations and organizational shifts.

Openly communicating leadership development goals with superiors, peers, and team members can foster a supportive environment that encourages goal achievement. This communication also invites feedback, which can provide valuable insights into how well the goals align with organizational expectations and how they might be adjusted for better alignment.

Aligning leadership development goals with personal values and organizational vision offers multiple benefits. It enhances the leader's sense of purpose and fulfillment, as they can see the direct impact of their growth on their personal career trajectory and the organization's success. Moreover, it fosters a more engaged and committed leadership approach, as leaders are more motivated when they work towards goals that resonate deeply with their values and contribute meaningfully to the organization's objectives.

The alignment of leadership development goals with personal values and organizational vision is a dynamic and ongoing process that requires reflection, communication, and adaptation. By pursuing this alignment, leaders can ensure that their development efforts yield not only personal satisfaction and growth but also significant contributions to the organization's strategic success.

Leadership competency models provide a structured framework for identifying the skills, behaviors, and attributes that contribute to effective leadership. These models are essential tools for both individuals and organizations aiming to assess leadership potential and pinpoint areas for development. By outlining specific competencies that are linked to successful leadership, these models offer a roadmap for personal growth and organizational development. Here is an overview of common leadership competency models and how they can be utilized to identify areas for development.

Common Leadership Competency Models

1. Emotional Intelligence Competency Model: Developed by Daniel Goleman, this model emphasizes the role of emotional intelligence in leadership effectiveness. It includes competencies such as self-awareness, self-regulation, motivation, empathy, and social skills. By assessing these areas, leaders can identify aspects of their emotional intelligence that need strengthening, such as improving their ability to manage stress or enhancing their empathetic engagement with team members.

2. Leadership Practices Inventory (LPI): This model focuses on behaviors that are essential to exemplary leadership, divided into five practices: Model the Way, Inspire a Shared Vision, Challenge the Process, Enable Others to Act, and Encourage the Heart. Leaders can use the LPI to evaluate their proficiency in these practices and identify specific actions they can take to improve, such as setting a stronger example for their team or finding more effective ways to motivate and recognize their contributions.

3. Situational Leadership Model: Centering on the adaptability of leadership styles, this model suggests that the most effective leaders adjust their approach based on the maturity and competency levels of their team members. Assessing leadership effectiveness through this lens can help leaders identify opportunities to better match their style to the needs of their team, ensuring more effective guidance and support.

4. Transformational Leadership Model: This model outlines components of leadership that inspire and drive change within organizations, including idealized influence, inspirational motivation, intellectual stimulation, and individualized consideration. Leaders can assess their capabilities in these areas to identify how they might more effectively inspire and engage their team, foster innovation, and address the individual needs of team members.

How to Use Leadership Competency Models for Assessment

- Self-Assessment and Reflection: Leaders can use these models as a basis for self-assessment, reflecting on their own behaviors and the feedback they have received from others to identify strengths and areas for improvement.

- 360-Degree Feedback: Incorporating questions related to these competencies in 360-degree feedback instruments allows leaders to gain insights from a wide range of perspectives, including peers, supervisors, and direct reports.

- Development Planning: Based on the assessment results, leaders can create targeted development plans that focus on enhancing specific competencies. This might involve seeking out training programs, finding mentorship opportunities, or setting specific, measurable goals related to improving their leadership practices.

- Continuous Monitoring and Evaluation: Leadership development is an ongoing process. Regularly revisiting these competency models and conducting follow-up assessments can help leaders track their progress and make necessary adjustments to their development plans.

Leadership competency models are invaluable tools for understanding the complex nature of effective leadership and identifying targeted areas for personal and professional growth. By leveraging these models for assessment and development planning, leaders can enhance their effectiveness and make meaningful contributions to their organizations.

Psychometric assessments are a critical component in the arsenal of leadership development tools, offering valuable insights into an individual's personality traits, cognitive abilities, emotional intelligence, and behavioral styles. These tools serve a variety of purposes, from helping to identify potential leaders and their development needs to enhancing self-awareness and facilitating team building. Understanding the different types of psychometric tools available, their purposes, and how to interpret their results can significantly enhance leadership assessment efforts.

Types of Psychometric Tools for Leadership Assessment

1. Personality Inventories: These assessments, such as the Myers-Briggs Type Indicator (MBTI) or the Big Five Personality Traits model, provide insights into an individual's personality characteristics and how these traits may influence their leadership style. Personality inventories can help leaders understand their preferences in communication, problem-solving, and decision-making.

2. Emotional Intelligence (EI) Assessments: Tools like the Emotional Quotient Inventory (EQ-i) measure aspects of emotional intelligence, including self-awareness, empathy, and social skills. EI assessments are particularly useful for identifying strengths and areas for improvement in managing emotions and fostering effective interpersonal relationships.

3. Cognitive Ability Tests: Assessments like the General Aptitude Test Battery (GATB) evaluate cognitive abilities such as verbal reasoning, numerical ability, and abstract thinking. These tests can help identify leaders with the intellectual capacity to process complex information, strategize, and solve problems effectively.

4. Behavioral Style Assessments: Tools such as the DiSC profile or the Thomas-Kilmann Conflict Mode Instrument (TKI) assess an individual's preferred behaviors in various situations, including leadership, communication, and conflict resolution. Understanding one's behavioral style can aid in developing more adaptive and flexible leadership approaches.

Psychometric assessments serve multiple critical purposes in the realm of leadership, each contributing to the overarching goal of enhancing organizational performance and leadership quality. In the context of selection and placement, these assessments are invaluable for identifying individuals who possess the innate potential and requisite skills for leadership roles. By aligning individual strengths with the specific needs of the organization, companies can ensure that leadership positions are filled by those most equipped to succeed in them. For development, psychometric assessments play a pivotal role by illuminating areas where individual leaders can grow. This insight lays the groundwork for creating targeted leadership development plans tailored to each leader's unique needs, fostering personal and professional growth.

In team-building efforts, understanding the diverse dynamics within a team becomes simpler with psychometric assessments. These tools shed light on the variety of styles and strengths present within a group, facilitating a deeper understanding that can be leveraged to enhance team collaboration and overall effectiveness. Additionally, in the crucial process of succession planning, psychometric assessments assist organizations in the early identification and meticulous preparation of future leaders. This proactive approach ensures that transitions in leadership are smooth and that the organization continues to thrive without interruption, maintaining continuity and stability. Collectively, these purposes underscore the integral role psychometric assessments play in cultivating effective leadership and fostering organizational success.

Interpreting the results from psychometric assessments demands a sophisticated and thoughtful approach, as these results represent just a fraction of the comprehensive landscape of leadership evaluation. It's imperative to situate the findings within the broader context of the individual's specific role, the prevailing culture within the organization, and any unique challenges that may be encountered. This holistic perspective enables a more meaningful understanding of the assessment outcomes. A critical step involves discerning distinct strengths that can be further harnessed, alongside pinpointing areas ripe for development, thus tailoring the focus of enhancement efforts more effectively.

The insights gleaned from these assessments are instrumental in shaping actionable leadership development plans. Such plans are grounded in setting precise objectives and formulating strategies aimed at fostering growth and improvement. Moreover, the complexity of interpreting psychometric assessment results often necessitates the involvement of professionals trained in psychology. Their expertise ensures that the process is conducted with the necessary accuracy and adheres to ethical standards.

When the process of selecting appropriate psychometric tools, fully grasping their intended purposes, and accurately interpreting the results is approached with diligence and care, it significantly augments leadership assessment and development initiatives. This meticulous process empowers both organizations and individuals to make well-informed decisions regarding leadership capacities and potential, thereby facilitating both personal advancement and the achievement of organizational goals.

Developmental assessments are specialized tools crafted to gauge the specific developmental needs of individuals, highlighting potential gaps in skills and knowledge that might hinder their effectiveness in their roles or their growth potential. Unlike performance evaluations, which often focus on past achievements and shortcomings, developmental assessments aim to paint a picture of where an individual currently stands in terms of their professional capabilities and where they need to venture for further growth.

These assessments take into account a wide array of factors, from cognitive abilities and emotional intelligence to specific job-related skills and leadership competencies. By identifying areas where an individual may lack critical knowledge or skills, developmental assessments provide a roadmap for targeted learning and growth. This approach not only benefits the individual by offering a clear path to personal and professional development but also aids organizations in crafting more focused and effective training and development programs.

In conducting developmental assessments, a variety of methods may be employed, including self-assessments, peer reviews, supervisor feedback, and more structured tools like 360-degree feedback surveys or psychometric tests. These tools work collectively to offer a comprehensive view of an individual's strengths and areas for improvement, considering not only the self-perception of the individual but also how they are viewed by others within the organization.

The ultimate goal of developmental assessments is to foster an environment of continuous learning and improvement. By clearly identifying developmental needs, these assessments empower individuals to take charge of their growth, seeking out education, training, and experiences that will bridge their knowledge and skills gaps. For organizations, understanding the developmental needs of their employees enables more strategic planning of professional development initiatives, ensuring that resources are invested in areas that will yield the highest return in terms of employee performance and satisfaction, as well as organizational effectiveness. In essence, developmental assessments serve as a critical tool in the ongoing process of learning and development, supporting individuals and organizations alike in their pursuit of excellence.

The application of assessment and goal setting in leadership development is a strategic process that culminates in the creation of a Personal Development Plan (PDP). This plan serves as a blueprint for an individual's growth journey, integrating insights from various assessments with SMART goals to outline a clear, actionable path for enhancing leadership competencies. Here's a step-by-step guide on how to craft a comprehensive leadership development plan:

1. Start with Self-Assessment and Feedback: Begin by conducting a thorough self-assessment of your leadership skills, behaviors, and effectiveness. Complement this self-evaluation with feedback from others, such as through 360-degree feedback, performance reviews, or informal feedback mechanisms. This dual approach provides a balanced view of your strengths and areas for development.

2. Analyze Assessment Results: Carefully analyze the results from the assessments and feedback, identifying key themes, strengths to be leveraged, and specific areas needing improvement. Consider how these findings align with your

personal values and the strategic objectives of your organization. This analysis forms the foundation of your development plan.

3. Set SMART Goals: Based on the insights gained from the assessments, set SMART goals for your leadership development. Each goal should be Specific, Measurable, Achievable, Relevant to your leadership role and personal aspirations, and Time-bound with a clear deadline. Ensure that these goals address both the areas for improvement identified in the assessments and the competencies critical for your current and future leadership roles.

4. Outline Strategies and Actions: For each SMART goal, outline specific strategies and actions required to achieve it. This might include participating in training programs, seeking mentorship or coaching, taking on new projects to gain experience, or practicing new behaviors in your daily leadership practice. Be as detailed as possible, assigning timelines and identifying resources or support needed for each action.

5. Implement and Monitor: With your plan in place, begin implementing the outlined strategies and actions. It's crucial to regularly monitor your progress towards each goal, adjusting your plan as necessary based on what's working and what's not. Keeping a journal or log can be helpful for tracking experiences, reflections, and learnings along the way.

6. Seek Feedback and Reflect: Continuously seek feedback on your development efforts from peers, supervisors, and direct reports. This ongoing feedback loop can provide valuable insights into your progress and areas needing further attention. Additionally, take time for regular self-reflection to assess your growth, challenges faced, and adjustments needed in your approach.

7. Revise and Update Your Plan: Leadership development is an ongoing process. As you achieve your goals, encounter new

challenges, or experience changes in your role or organizational context, revisit and update your Personal Development Plan. This iterative process ensures your development efforts remain aligned with your evolving leadership journey and the needs of your organization.

By systematically integrating assessment results and SMART goals into a Personal Development Plan, leaders can ensure their growth efforts are focused, strategic, and aligned with their personal and professional objectives. This structured approach to leadership development not only facilitates individual growth but also contributes to the overall effectiveness and success of the organization.

Monitoring progress and adjusting goals are critical steps in the leadership development process. These practices ensure that development efforts remain relevant, effective, and aligned with changing personal aspirations and organizational needs. Here are tips for effectively reviewing progress, incorporating feedback, and making necessary adjustments to development plans:

- Set Regular Review Intervals: Establish a regular schedule for reviewing your progress towards each goal in your Personal Development Plan. This could be monthly, quarterly, or at another interval that makes sense given your goals and timelines. Consistency in review helps keep your development efforts on track and allows for timely adjustments.

- Use a Structured Review Process: Approach each review session with a structured process in mind. Assess what has been accomplished since the last review, what challenges were encountered, and what can be learned from these experiences. Evaluate whether each goal remains relevant and achievable within the set timelines.

- Gather and Incorporate Feedback: Feedback from peers, supervisors, direct reports, and mentors is invaluable in assessing your progress. Actively seek feedback on areas related to your development goals, asking for specific examples of behaviors observed and suggestions for improvement. Reflect on this feedback during your review sessions to gain additional insights into your progress and areas needing more focus.

- Measure Against Specific Criteria: For each goal, have clear criteria for what success looks like. Use these criteria to objectively measure your progress. This might include specific competencies developed, behaviors demonstrated, or outcomes achieved, depending on the nature of the goal.

- Adjust Goals and Actions as Needed: Based on your review and the feedback received, be prepared to make adjustments to your goals and the actions planned to achieve them. This might involve redefining goals, extending timelines, or changing strategies if certain approaches are not yielding the expected results. Flexibility is key to responding to new challenges and opportunities that arise.

- Document Changes and Rationale: Keep a record of any changes made to your goals or development plan, including the rationale for these adjustments. This documentation can be helpful for future reference and for sharing your development journey with mentors or supervisors who are supporting your growth.

- Celebrate Achievements: Acknowledge and celebrate milestones and achievements along the way. Recognizing your progress not only boosts motivation but also reinforces the behaviors and efforts that led to success, making them more likely to be repeated.

- Reflect on the Learning Process: Beyond assessing progress towards specific goals, reflect on what the process of working towards these goals has taught you about yourself as a leader and learner. This meta-cognition can be incredibly valuable for your ongoing development.

By regularly reviewing progress, incorporating feedback, and making necessary adjustments to your development plan, you can ensure that your leadership development efforts are dynamic, responsive, and tailored to your evolving needs and circumstances. This iterative process supports sustained growth and development, enabling you to achieve your full potential as a leader.

The journey of leadership development is both demanding and rewarding, underscored by the critical processes of assessment and goal setting. These foundational elements not only provide a structured approach to identifying strengths and areas for growth but also pave a clear path for targeted improvement and personal evolution. As we have explored, the significance of these processes in the context of leadership development cannot be overstated; they are essential for any leader seeking to enhance their effectiveness, adaptability, and impact within an organization.

Leaders are encouraged to embrace continuous self-assessment and goal refinement as integral components of their development journey. This ongoing engagement with one's growth process ensures that leadership capabilities are not only maintained but also expanded in response to new challenges, opportunities, and shifts in organizational direction. The act of regularly evaluating one's progress, soliciting feedback, and adjusting goals accordingly fosters a dynamic and responsive approach to personal and professional development.

The transformative potential of a well-structured development plan, grounded in realistic and challenging goals, is immense. Such a plan, informed by thorough assessment and SMART goal-setting, equips leaders with the focus, direction, and motivation needed to pursue their growth with intention and purpose. It allows leaders to translate insights and aspirations into actionable steps, leading to measurable improvements in leadership competencies and behaviors. Moreover, a development plan that is closely aligned with both personal values and organizational objectives ensures that the leader's growth contributes to broader organizational success.

In closing, the processes of assessment and goal setting are not just administrative tasks to be checked off a list. They are opportunities for reflection, learning, and transformation. By committing to these processes, leaders can navigate their development journey with confidence, supported by a clear understanding of where they are, where they want to be, and how they plan to get there. The result is not only enhanced leadership effectiveness but also a deeper sense of fulfillment and purpose in one's role. As such, leaders at all levels are encouraged to view their development plans not as static documents, but as living frameworks that guide their continuous growth and adaptation in the ever-evolving landscape of leadership.

Exercises for Chapter 4:

Assessment and Goal Setting

Exercise 9: Completing the Leadership Assessment Using Provided Tools

This exercise is designed to encourage readers to engage actively in self-assessment, utilizing the tools provided in this chapter and accessible online. The aim is to gain a deeper understanding of your current leadership competencies and identify areas for growth.

Instructions:

1. Select Assessment Tools: Choose one or more of the assessment tools recommended in this chapter. Consider tools that measure a range of competencies, including emotional intelligence, leadership styles, and decision-making abilities.

2. Prepare for the Assessment: Before beginning the assessment, ensure you are in a quiet space where you can reflect honestly on your behaviors and experiences. Approach the assessment with an open mind, ready to embrace insights about your leadership.

3. Complete the Assessment: Follow the instructions for each selected tool carefully. Answer each question as honestly as possible, based on your recent experiences in leadership roles.

4. Reflect on Your Results: Once you have completed the assessments, spend time reflecting on the results. Note any surprises or confirmations about your leadership competencies.

5. Identify your strengths and areas where there is room for improvement.

6. Document Your Insights: Write down key takeaways from your assessment results. Highlight specific competencies you excel in and those you wish to develop further.

7. Seek Feedback: If possible, discuss your assessment results with a mentor, coach, or trusted colleague. External perspectives can provide additional insights and help validate your self-assessment.

Exercise10: Setting Personal SMART Goals

Based on the outcomes of your leadership assessments, this exercise will guide you through setting your own SMART goals for leadership development. These goals will be Specific, Measurable, Achievable, Relevant, and Time-bound.

Instructions:

1. Review Your Assessment Insights: Begin by reviewing the key areas for development identified in your leadership assessments. Consider which areas are most critical for your growth as a leader.

2. Brainstorm Potential Goals: List potential goals related to these areas of development. Think about what you aim to achieve in your leadership journey.

3. Craft SMART Goals: Refine your list into SMART goals. For each goal, ensure it is:

4. Specific: Clearly define what you want to accomplish.

5. Measurable: Identify how you will measure progress and success.

6. Achievable: Ensure the goal is attainable with effort.
7. Relevant: Confirm the goal aligns with your leadership role and personal growth aspirations.

8. Time-bound: Set a realistic deadline for achieving the goal.

9. Develop an Action Plan: For each SMART goal, outline specific actions you will take to achieve it. Include resources you will need, potential obstacles, and strategies for overcoming them.

10. Commit to Regular Reviews: Set a schedule for reviewing your progress towards each goal. Regular check-ins will help you stay on track and make adjustments as needed.

11. Document Your Goals and Plan: Keep a written record of your

12. SMART goals and action plans. This documentation will serve as a roadmap for your leadership development journey.

By completing these exercises, you will have taken significant steps toward understanding your current leadership competencies and setting a clear, actionable path for your development. Engaging in regular self-assessment and goal refinement is essential for continuous growth and achieving leadership excellence.

Chapter 5: Developing Executive Leadership Skills

In the dynamic and ever-evolving world of executive leadership, the continuous development of key leadership skills is not just beneficial—it's essential. As the challenges and complexities of leading organizations grow, so too does the need for executives to refine and expand their repertoire of skills. This chapter delves into the critical areas of leadership skill development that are fundamental to executive effectiveness and organizational success. By focusing on enhancing communication and interpersonal skills, honing strategic thinking and problem-solving capabilities, and mastering the art of influence and negotiation, leaders can ensure they are well-equipped to navigate the demands of their roles and drive their organizations forward.

The importance of continuously developing leadership skills cannot be overstated. In an environment marked by rapid change and intense competition, the ability of executives to adapt and grow is a significant determinant of organizational resilience and success. Effective leadership goes beyond the ability to manage operations; it encompasses inspiring and motivating teams, envisioning and executing strategies, and forging beneficial relationships both within and outside the organization.

This section is dedicated to exploring the nuances of these essential leadership skills. We begin with communication and interpersonal skills, emphasizing the role of clear, empathetic, and effective communication in building trust, fostering collaboration, and ensuring alignment across teams. Next, we turn our attention to strategic thinking and problem-solving capabilities, where we examine how executives can cultivate a forward-looking mindset, identify opportunities for innovation, and navigate complex challenges with agility and insight. Finally, we explore the strategies and techniques that can enhance an executive's ability to influence others and negotiate successfully, skills that are critical in achieving organizational goals.

Effective communication is the cornerstone of successful leadership, especially in the executive realm where the stakes are high and the impact is far-reaching. At its core, effective communication encompasses several key elements: clarity, conciseness, and active listening, each playing a pivotal role in ensuring that messages are not only delivered but also understood and acted upon as intended.

Clarity is essential in communication, particularly in complex organizational settings where ambiguity can lead to confusion and inefficiency. Clarity involves expressing ideas in a straightforward manner, using language that is accessible to the audience without oversimplification. It's about making sure the message is unambiguous and that the intent behind the communication is clear to all involved. This requires executives to be mindful of their word choice, structure of their messages, and the medium through which they communicate, tailoring their approach to fit the context and the audience.

Conciseness is equally important, as it respects the recipient's time and attention. In an executive context, time is a precious commodity, and the ability to convey essential information succinctly without omitting crucial details is a valuable skill. Conciseness helps in maintaining the focus of the communication, making it easier for the audience to grasp the key points and take necessary actions. This does not mean important information should be left out; rather, it's about being strategic in what to include and what to omit, ensuring the message remains impactful and direct.

Active Listening goes hand in hand with effective verbal communication. It's the practice of fully concentrating on what is being said rather than just passively 'hearing' the message of the speaker. Active listening involves giving full attention to the speaker, understanding their message, responding appropriately, and then remembering what was said. It's a critical skill for executives, as it facilitates better understanding, helps in gathering insights, and shows respect for the contributors, thereby enhancing interpersonal relations and fostering a culture of openness and trust.

The role of emotional intelligence in enhancing communication and interpersonal relations cannot be overstated. Emotional intelligence—the ability to understand and manage one's own emotions as well as recognize and influence the emotions of others—plays a crucial role in effective communication. It enables executives to tailor their messages based on the emotional state, needs, and preferences of their audience. This sensitivity to emotions helps in delivering messages in a way that is more likely to be positively received and acted upon. Additionally, emotional intelligence facilitates empathy, allowing leaders to establish deeper connections with their teams, understand their perspectives better, and communicate in a way that motivates and inspires.

Mastering the fundamentals of effective communication—clarity, conciseness, active listening, coupled with a high degree of emotional intelligence—is indispensable for executive leaders. These elements work synergistically to enhance not only the efficiency of communication but also its effectiveness in fostering strong relationships, driving alignment, and achieving organizational goals. As such, executives are encouraged to continuously develop and refine these skills as part of their leadership development journey.

Building and maintaining relationships are critical competencies for executive leaders, enabling them to establish trust, foster collaboration, and navigate the complexities of organizational dynamics effectively. The foundation of strong relationships in the workplace is trust and rapport, which can be nurtured through consistent, transparent, and empathetic interactions. Here, we explore strategies and techniques for cultivating these essential elements, managing conflicts, and facilitating collaborative problem-solving.

Strategies for Building Trust and Rapport

- Consistent Communication: Regular and open communication is vital. Keeping teams, peers, and stakeholders informed about developments, decisions, and challenges demonstrates transparency and fosters trust. It's equally important to create channels for two-way communication, allowing others to share their insights and concerns.

- Demonstrate Integrity and Reliability: Actions speak louder than words. Consistently following through on commitments and standing by your values, even in challenging situations, reinforces your reliability and integrity, thereby building trust.

- Personalized Interactions: Take the time to get to know the individuals you work with. Understanding their career aspirations, strengths, and even personal interests can go a long way in building rapport. Tailoring your interaction style to match the preferences of different team members and stakeholders can also enhance mutual respect and understanding.

- Acknowledge and Appreciate Contributions: Recognizing the efforts and achievements of team members and peers not only boosts morale but also strengthens relationships. Genuine appreciation fosters a positive work environment and encourages continued contribution and engagement.

Techniques for Managing Conflicts and Facilitating Collaborative Problem-Solving

- Active Listening and Empathy: When conflicts arise, practice active listening to understand the perspectives and feelings of all parties involved. Demonstrating empathy towards differing viewpoints can help de-escalate tensions and open the door to constructive dialogue.

- Seek Common Ground: Focus on identifying shared goals or interests as a foundation for resolution. By highlighting common objectives, you can shift the conversation from opposing positions to collaborative problem-solving.

- Use Structured Problem-Solving Methods: Implementing structured approaches, such as brainstorming sessions or the "Five Whys" technique, can guide the group towards creative solutions. Encouraging participation from all parties ensures diverse perspectives are considered, enhancing the quality of the solution.

- Negotiate and Compromise: Sometimes, resolving conflicts requires negotiation and compromise. Approach these situations with a willingness to find a middle ground that respects the needs and limitations of all parties involved.

- Follow Up and Support Implementation: After a resolution is reached, follow up to ensure agreements are implemented effectively. Providing ongoing support and addressing any subsequent issues promptly can prevent conflicts from re-emerging and reinforce a culture of trust and collaboration.

Building and maintaining strong relationships require a deliberate and sustained effort. By employing these strategies and techniques, executive leaders can create an environment of trust, respect, and cooperation. Such an environment not only enhances team and organizational performance but also contributes to a more engaging and fulfilling work experience for everyone involved.

Developing a strategic mindset is crucial for executive leaders tasked with navigating complex business environments and driving their organizations toward a compelling vision. Strategic thinking enables leaders to step back from the day-to-day operations and focus on the bigger picture, anticipating future trends, challenges, and opportunities. This mindset is not just about planning for the future; it's about creating it, making informed decisions that propel the organization forward in a meaningful and deliberate way.

The importance of strategic thinking lies in its ability to provide clarity and direction in an increasingly volatile and uncertain business landscape. Leaders with a strategic mindset are better equipped to align their organization's resources and capabilities with its long-term goals, ensuring sustainability and competitive advantage. They see beyond immediate challenges, focusing instead on developing strategies that foster long-term growth, innovation, and resilience.

Cultivating a forward-looking perspective requires leaders to be proactive rather than reactive. It involves constantly scanning the external environment for trends, technological advancements, and shifts in consumer behavior that could impact the organization. This external focus, combined with a deep understanding of the organization's internal strengths and weaknesses, allows leaders to identify potential opportunities for growth and areas of vulnerability that need to be addressed.

Techniques for developing a strategic mindset include:

1. Engage in Continuous Learning: Stay informed about industry trends, emerging technologies, and global economic factors. This knowledge can help you anticipate changes and adapt your strategies accordingly.

2. Practice Scenario Planning: Regularly engage in scenario planning exercises to envision different future states based on varying trends and uncertainties. This can help you prepare for a range of possibilities and develop more flexible strategies.

3. Foster Cross-Functional Collaboration: Encourage collaboration across different departments and disciplines within your organization. Diverse perspectives can spark innovative ideas and provide insights that might not be apparent from a single vantage point.

4. Allocate Time for Strategic Thinking: Schedule regular time away from day-to-day tasks to reflect on your organization's

strategic direction. Use this time to review your strategic plans, assess progress, and adjust course as needed.

5. Seek Feedback and Challenge Assumptions: Open yourself up to feedback from peers, mentors, and other stakeholders. Be willing to challenge your assumptions and consider alternative viewpoints to refine your strategic thinking.

By embracing these techniques, leaders can enhance their ability to think strategically and navigate their organizations through the complexities of the modern business environment. Developing a strategic mindset is an ongoing process, one that requires dedication, curiosity, and the willingness to embrace change. As leaders cultivate this mindset, they not only drive their organizations toward achieving their vision but also contribute to a culture that values foresight, innovation, and strategic agility.

Systematic approaches to problem-solving empower executives to tackle challenges methodically, ensuring solutions are not just immediate fixes but sustainable over the long term. Root cause analysis and creative thinking techniques stand out as two fundamental strategies in the executive toolkit, each offering a unique pathway to uncovering and addressing the underlying issues of complex problems.

Root cause analysis is a methodical technique used to identify the underlying reasons for a problem. It involves examining the symptoms of an issue to trace it back to its origin, allowing leaders to address the core of the problem rather than its surface manifestations. This approach often employs tools like the "Five Whys" technique, where asking "why" repeatedly helps peel back the layers of a problem, revealing its root cause. By focusing on the root cause, executives can implement solutions that are more likely to prevent the problem from recurring, enhancing the resilience and efficiency of their operations.

On the other hand, creative thinking techniques, such as brainstorming, mind mapping, and lateral thinking, encourage looking at problems from new angles and exploring innovative solutions. These techniques challenge conventional wisdom and encourage divergent thinking, making it possible to find novel solutions to stubborn or complex problems. Creative thinking is particularly valuable in situations where traditional approaches have failed or where the landscape is rapidly changing, requiring a fresh perspective and adaptive solutions. Illustrative of these approaches are case studies from the executive world.

Case Study 1: Root Cause Analysis in Manufacturing: A manufacturing company faced recurring equipment failures that slowed production. Initial fixes were only temporarily effective. The leadership team conducted a root cause analysis and discovered that the real issue was not equipment quality but inadequate training for operators. By addressing the root cause with comprehensive training programs, the company not only resolved the equipment issues but also improved overall operational efficiency.

Case Study 2: Creative Thinking in Product Development: Facing stagnation in its product line, a technology company used creative thinking workshops to rejuvenate its approach to product development. By encouraging team members to think outside industry norms and consider unconventional customer needs, the company successfully developed a new product that opened up an untapped market segment, driving significant growth.

These case studies underscore the effectiveness of systematic problem-solving approaches in executive scenarios. Root cause analysis ensures that solutions are targeted and enduring, while creative thinking techniques unlock innovation and adaptability. For executives, mastering these approaches means being able to navigate the complexities of their roles with confidence, ensuring not just the resolution of immediate issues but the long-term success and sustainability of their organizations. The integration of these problem-solving strategies into daily decision-making processes can transform challenges into opportunities for growth and innovation.

The psychology of influence plays a crucial role in leadership, offering insights into how leaders can guide and inspire action within their teams and organizations. By understanding and applying the principles of influence, leaders can ethically leverage their ability to affect the ideas, behaviors, and actions of others, fostering a culture of motivation, engagement, and collective achievement. Influence in leadership is not about coercion or manipulation but about persuading and inspiring others towards a shared vision or goal. Key principles such as reciprocity, commitment and consistency, social proof, authority, liking, and scarcity, when applied thoughtfully and ethically, enhance a leader's ability to motivate their team, drive organizational change, and navigate stakeholder engagement effectively.

Applying these principles involves building genuine relationships to establish trust and rapport, making influence more naturally accepted. Transparent communication shares information openly, enhancing trust and rallying others around common goals. Empowering others by encouraging autonomy and recognizing contributions motivates individuals and reinforces positive behavior. Leaders can also model the behavior they wish to see, leading by example to encourage others to emulate successful actions and attitudes. Additionally, fostering collaboration and consensus by engaging team members in decision-making processes builds commitment and leverages the group's collective wisdom.

The effective use of influence in leadership is about connecting with, motivating, and empowering others, not to manipulate but to genuinely guide change and achieve organizational objectives. The principles of influence, grounded in the psychology of human behavior, are integral to effective leadership, enabling leaders to inspire action and foster an environment where individuals and the organization can flourish together.

Negotiation skills are indispensable for leaders, enabling them to navigate complex interactions and achieve outcomes that benefit both their organization and other parties involved. Mastering key negotiation techniques not only facilitates the reaching of agreements but also strengthens relationships and fosters collaboration. To achieve win-win outcomes in organizational settings, leaders must employ a blend of strategic approaches, underscored by thorough preparation, active listening, and empathy.

At the heart of effective negotiation lies the principle of seeking mutual benefit. Leaders who approach negotiations with the aim of finding solutions that satisfy both parties' core interests are more likely to foster goodwill and long-term partnerships. Techniques such as identifying shared goals, emphasizing common interests, and exploring options for mutual gain are central to this approach. By focusing on interests rather than positions, leaders can navigate beyond surface-level demands to understand the underlying needs of all parties, opening the door to creative and collaborative solutions.

Preparation is a critical component of successful negotiation. Before entering negotiations, leaders should invest time in understanding their own objectives, the interests and potential constraints of the other party, and the context in which the negotiation takes place. This preparation involves gathering relevant information, defining clear goals, and considering alternative outcomes. Being well-prepared not only boosts a leader's confidence but also enables them to articulate their position more effectively and anticipate the needs and objections of the other party.

Active listening is another vital skill in negotiations. It involves fully concentrating on what the other party is saying, understanding their message, and responding thoughtfully. Active listening demonstrates respect and openness, building trust and facilitating clearer communication. It allows leaders to pick up on nuances and use the insights gained to steer the negotiation in a direction that addresses the concerns and aspirations of all involved.

Empathy plays a crucial role in understanding the perspectives and emotions of the other party. By empathizing with their situation, leaders can better navigate emotional undercurrents and address any resistance or concerns. Empathy helps in crafting proposals that are more likely to be received positively, as they take into account the interests and feelings of the other party.

Negotiation skills are essential for leaders seeking to achieve win-win outcomes in organizational contexts. Key negotiation techniques, underscored by preparation, active listening, and empathy, equip leaders to engage in constructive dialogue, overcome impasses, and forge agreements that are beneficial for all parties involved. Through effective negotiation, leaders can resolve conflicts, secure resources, and build the partnerships necessary for organizational success.

Creating a Personal Skill Development Plan involves a thoughtful process of self-assessment, goal setting, and strategic action to enhance key leadership skills such as communication, strategic thinking, and influencing. This plan serves as a roadmap for leaders aiming to elevate their effectiveness and adaptability in an ever-changing business landscape.

The journey begins with a comprehensive self-assessment and the gathering of feedback from peers, supervisors, and direct reports to gain a holistic view of one's current capabilities and areas needing improvement. Based on this feedback, leaders can pinpoint specific, actionable development goals for each key skill area. It's crucial that these goals are framed to be SMART—specific, measurable, achievable, relevant, and time-bound—to ensure clarity and facilitate achievement.

For each identified goal, a detailed strategy outlining the steps necessary for skill enhancement is essential. This could involve enrolling in targeted workshops or courses, engaging with a mentor or coach who has demonstrated excellence in these areas, or finding opportunities within one's role to practice and refine these skills. Establishing clear milestones and timelines for each goal aids in maintaining focus and momentum, allowing for regular assessment and adjustments along the way.

Ongoing skill enhancement is further supported through formal training opportunities, such as workshops, courses, and seminars that focus on advanced communication techniques, strategic thinking frameworks, and effective influencing strategies. Accessing online platforms and executive education programs offered by business schools can provide valuable learning experiences.

Mentoring and coaching relationships offer personalized guidance and insights from experienced leaders, creating an accountability mechanism that encourages continuous progress. Practical application of developing skills in real-world scenarios, such as leading strategic projects, negotiating, or delivering presentations, is critical for solidifying learning and building confidence.

Peer learning, through participation in study groups or professional networks, allows for the exchange of experiences, challenges, and strategies, offering additional support and perspective. Continuous reflection on learning experiences and the outcomes of developmental efforts, coupled with the willingness to adjust the development plan based on evolving insights and feedback, ensures the plan remains relevant and effective.

The creation and execution of a Personal Skill Development Plan is a proactive approach to leadership development. By methodically enhancing communication, strategic thinking, and influencing skills, leaders can ensure they remain well-equipped to navigate the complexities of their roles, driving personal growth and organizational success.

Monitoring and evaluating progress in leadership skill development is an essential process that ensures continuous growth and adaptability. This involves employing a variety of techniques to assess improvements, gather feedback, and engage in self-reflection, enabling leaders to make informed adjustments to their development plans. By systematically tracking progress and remaining responsive to feedback, leaders can refine their approach to development, ensuring their efforts align with their goals and the evolving needs of their organization.

One effective technique for assessing improvements is setting up regular review sessions. These sessions can be used to evaluate progress against the specific, measurable goals outlined in the development plan. During these reviews, leaders can examine evidence of skill enhancement, such as feedback from colleagues, performance metrics, and personal reflections on recent challenges and achievements. This structured approach allows for a clear assessment of which areas have seen growth and where further development is needed.

Incorporating feedback from a variety of sources is another critical component of monitoring progress. This feedback can come from direct reports, peers, supervisors, and mentors, providing diverse perspectives on the leader's performance and impact. Leaders can solicit feedback through formal mechanisms, such as performance reviews or 360-degree feedback processes, as well as through informal conversations. Actively seeking and being open to feedback encourages a culture of continuous improvement and helps leaders identify blind spots in their development.

Self-reflection plays a pivotal role in evaluating leadership growth. By regularly taking time to reflect on their experiences, decisions, and interactions, leaders can gain deeper insights into their own behaviors, identify patterns, and recognize areas of success and challenge. Reflection can be facilitated through journaling, meditation, or discussions with a coach or mentor. This introspective process allows leaders to critically assess their development journey, integrating their own perceptions with external feedback to form a comprehensive view of their progress.

Based on the outcomes of these assessments, feedback, and reflections, leaders are equipped to make necessary adjustments to their development plans. This might involve re-prioritizing goals, adopting new strategies for skill enhancement, or seeking additional resources and support. The ability to adapt the development plan in response to feedback and self-assessment ensures that leaders continue to grow in ways that are both personally meaningful and aligned with organizational objectives.

Monitoring and evaluating progress in leadership development is a dynamic and iterative process. By employing techniques such as regular review sessions, incorporating diverse feedback, and engaging in self-reflection, leaders can ensure their development efforts remain focused, relevant, and effective. This ongoing commitment to assessing and adjusting their approach to development allows leaders to achieve sustained growth, enhancing their leadership skills and contributing to the success of their teams and organizations.

In exploring the landscape of executive leadership, we've delved into the critical skills that underpin effective leadership: communication, strategic thinking, influencing, and the foundational practices of assessment, goal setting, and continuous skill development. These competencies are not merely advantageous but essential for navigating the complexities of today's business environment, driving organizational success, and fostering meaningful professional relationships.

The continuous development of these skills is paramount. As the business world evolves, so too must the capabilities of its leaders. The journey of leadership development is ongoing, marked by a commitment to self-improvement, adaptability, and the pursuit of excellence. Leaders who dedicate themselves to refining these skills are better equipped to inspire their teams, navigate challenges, and seize opportunities with insight and agility.

Readers are encouraged to actively engage in the exercises provided throughout this discussion. These exercises are designed not only to offer insights into your current leadership abilities but also to illuminate areas for growth. By participating in these structured activities, you can set a course for your development that is both intentional and impactful, tailored to your unique strengths and the specific demands of your leadership role.

The journey of leadership development is, at its heart, a continuous process of learning, adaptation, and growth. It is a path marked by challenges, yes, but also by immense rewards. As you engage with this process, remember that the pursuit of leadership excellence is not a destination but a journey—one that demands resilience, curiosity, and the willingness to grow. Through continuous self-assessment, goal refinement, and skill development, you can forge a style of leadership that is not only effective but also authentic and sustainable.

Let this exploration serve as both a guide and an inspiration on your leadership development journey. The path to leadership excellence is ongoing, and each step forward is a step toward realizing your full potential as a leader. Embrace the journey with an open mind and a committed heart, ready to learn, adapt, and grow in ways that will not only enhance your leadership capabilities but also enrich your professional life and the lives of those you lead.

Exercises for Chapter 5: Developing Executive Leadership Skills

Exercise 11: Communication Style Inventory

This guided exercise is designed to help you identify your predominant communication style and understand its impact on your leadership approach. By recognizing your communication style, you can enhance your awareness of areas for improvement and learn how to adapt to the diverse communication preferences of your team and peers.

Step 1: Identify Your Communication Style

Begin by reflecting on your recent interactions in various settings—meetings, one-on-ones, email correspondence, and presentations. Consider the following descriptions of common communication styles:

- Assertive: You communicate your needs, ideas, and feelings clearly and directly while respecting others.

- Passive: You tend to prioritize the needs and preferences of others over your own, often avoiding confrontation.

- Aggressive: You express your thoughts and needs in a way that may infringe on the rights of others, often prioritizing your own outcomes over others'.

- Passive-Aggressive: You indirectly express negative feelings through your actions or non-verbal communication rather than addressing issues directly.

- Analytical: You rely heavily on data, facts, and logical reasoning in your communication, sometimes at the expense of emotional considerations.

Reflect on which style(s) most closely align with your typical way of communicating. It's possible to exhibit different styles in different contexts or with different people.

Step 2: Reflection Questions

After identifying your predominant communication style(s), consider the following questions to deepen your understanding and identify areas for growth:

1. How has my communication style impacted my leadership effectiveness? Consider both positive impacts and challenges.

2. In what situations has my communication style been particularly effective or ineffective? Reflect on specific instances and the outcomes.

3. How do the members of my team prefer to communicate, and how does this align with my style? Consider the diversity of communication preferences among your team members.

4. What adjustments can I make to my communication style to enhance my leadership approach? Think about strategies for adapting your style to different situations or individuals.

Step 3: Action Plan for Improvement

Based on your reflections, develop a brief action plan that outlines specific steps you can take to enhance your communication effectiveness. This might include:

- Seeking feedback from peers and team members on your communication style and its impact.

- Practicing active listening in your interactions to better understand others' perspectives.

- Engaging in training or workshops to develop skills that complement your existing communication style (e.g., assertiveness training for those with a passive style).

- Actively adapting your communication approach based on the context and audience to ensure your message is received as intended.

Step 4: Implementation and Review

Commit to implementing your action plan over the next few months. Schedule regular review periods to assess your progress, adjust your strategies as needed, and reflect on how changes in your communication style influence your leadership effectiveness.

By engaging in this Communication Style Inventory exercise, you take an important step towards becoming a more versatile and effective leader. Recognizing and adapting your communication style to meet the needs of your team and organizational context can significantly enhance your leadership impact and foster a more collaborative and productive work environment.

Exercise 12: Strategic Challenge Simulation

This interactive simulation exercise is designed to immerse you in a complex business scenario, challenging you to apply your strategic thinking and problem-solving skills. The goal is to navigate the scenario successfully by making informed decisions that reflect a deep understanding of the situation, the competitive landscape, and potential future implications. Following the simulation, a series of debrief questions will help you reflect on your decision-making process and the outcomes achieved.
Scenario Overview

Imagine you are the CEO of a mid-sized technology company, "Tech Innovate," that specializes in developing eco-friendly smart home devices. Recently, your main competitor launched a new product that significantly undercuts your prices, threatening your market share. Additionally, there's a growing trend in the market toward integrated home systems, a segment your current product line does not fully address. You need to decide how to respond to these challenges to secure your company's future growth and sustainability.

Simulation Steps

1. Market Analysis: Begin by conducting a comprehensive analysis of the current market conditions, customer preferences, and technological trends. Consider how these factors impact your strategic options.

2. Competitive Response: Decide how to respond to your competitor's pricing strategy. Options might include introducing a new product line, adjusting your pricing model, enhancing product features, or increasing marketing efforts.

3. Innovation and Development: Consider whether to invest in developing integrated home system solutions. Evaluate the potential risks and rewards, including the impact on your resources and existing product lines.

4. Stakeholder Engagement: Determine how you will communicate your strategy to stakeholders, including employees, investors, and customers. Consider their expectations and how to gain their support.

5. Implementation Plan: Outline a high-level plan for implementing your chosen strategy, including key actions, timelines, and milestones.

Debrief Questions

- After completing the simulation, reflect on your experience and decision-making process by considering the following questions:

- How did you approach the market analysis, and what key factors influenced your strategic decisions?

- What criteria did you use to select your competitive response and how confident are you in its effectiveness?

- In choosing whether to innovate and develop new solutions, how did you balance the potential for growth with the risks involved?

- How did you plan to engage with stakeholders, and why did you choose this approach?

- Looking back, how might different decisions have led to different outcomes? What would you do differently if faced with a similar scenario in the future?

- What insights have you gained about your strategic thinking and problem-solving skills, and how can you apply these learnings to real-world challenges?

This Strategic Challenge Simulation exercise is an opportunity to practice and refine your strategic thinking in a risk-free environment. By engaging deeply with the scenario and reflecting on your decision-making process, you can enhance your ability to navigate complex business challenges and drive your organization toward success.

Exercise 13: Negotiation Role-Play

This role-play exercise is structured to provide a practical, immersive experience in applying negotiation techniques within a leadership context. Through engaging with scenarios that reflect common challenges faced by executives, participants can hone their negotiation skills, explore different strategies, and receive feedback on their effectiveness. The exercise aims to enhance understanding of the negotiation process, improve the ability to reach mutually beneficial agreements, and reflect on the use of various negotiation tactics.

Scenario Setup

Participants are divided into pairs, with each pair given a negotiation scenario common in executive settings, such as negotiating a partnership agreement with another company, resolving a conflict between two departments, or securing resources for a new project from senior management. Each participant is assigned a role with specific objectives, constraints, and background information relevant to the scenario.

Negotiation Process

- Preparation: Each participant takes time to prepare for the negotiation, outlining their objectives, identifying their BATNA (Best Alternative to a Negotiated Agreement), and considering the interests and potential positions of the other party.

- Role-Play: Participants engage in the negotiation, applying techniques such as active listening, framing their arguments in terms of the other party's interests, and exploring creative options for mutual gain.

- Debrief: After the role-play, participants exchange feedback on their negotiation strategies and outcomes. This debrief focuses on what strategies were effective, what challenges were encountered, and how communication could have been improved.

Reflection Questions

Following the role-play and feedback session, participants reflect on their negotiation experience by considering the following questions:

1. How well did you prepare for the negotiation, and how did your preparation (or lack thereof) influence the outcome?

2. What negotiation techniques did you employ, and how effective were they in achieving your objectives?

3. How did you handle points of contention or resistance from the other party? Could these situations have been managed differently for a better outcome?

4. In what ways did the negotiation shift from competitive to collaborative, and what triggered these shifts?

5. Reflecting on the feedback received, what aspects of your negotiation approach would you like to improve or change for future negotiations?

6. How can the insights gained from this exercise be applied to real-world leadership challenges you currently face or may encounter?

The Negotiation Role-Play exercise provides a dynamic platform for practicing and refining negotiation skills in a safe and constructive environment. By actively engaging in the scenarios, receiving feedback, and reflecting on their negotiation strategies, participants can develop a deeper understanding of the complexities of negotiation and enhance their ability to lead and achieve objectives effectively in their professional roles.

Chapter 6: Performance Enhancement Strategies

The quest for performance enhancement is both a personal and organizational imperative. This chapter delves into the multifaceted concept of performance enhancement, underscoring its critical importance for leaders and their teams in achieving peak productivity and operational excellence. At the heart of performance enhancement lies the understanding that leadership effectiveness directly influences team dynamics, innovation, and the overall success of the organization. Therefore, executive leaders must continually seek ways to elevate their performance and, by extension, that of their teams.

Performance enhancement in leadership goes beyond mere incremental improvements; it encompasses a comprehensive approach that integrates feedback mechanisms, effective time management, and a steadfast commitment to fostering a culture of continuous learning. Each of these elements plays a pivotal role in driving performance improvements and, when combined, they create a powerful engine for organizational growth and success.

Feedback mechanisms serve as the cornerstone of performance enhancement, offering leaders and their teams valuable insights into their work's impact, areas for improvement, and opportunities for development. Constructive feedback, whether from peers, supervisors, or direct reports, provides a mirror reflecting current performance levels and illuminates the path toward greater effectiveness.

Time management, in its essence, is about maximizing the value of one's efforts and resources. For executive leaders, mastering time management means prioritizing tasks, delegating appropriately, and eliminating inefficiencies, thereby ensuring that both their time and that of their teams is spent on activities that directly contribute to achieving strategic objectives.

Cultivating a culture of continuous learning within the organization is perhaps the most transformative strategy for performance enhancement. This culture encourages openness to new ideas, adaptability, and the ongoing development of skills and knowledge. By fostering an environment where learning is valued and pursued, leaders not only enhance their own performance but also empower their teams to innovate, adapt, and excel in an ever-changing business landscape.

This chapter offers a comprehensive exploration of performance enhancement strategies tailored for executive leadership. Through a combination of leveraging feedback, mastering time management, and nurturing a culture of continuous learning, leaders can unlock their full potential and guide their organizations toward sustained success and competitiveness.

In the landscape of leadership development and team performance enhancement, constructive feedback emerges as a pivotal tool. Its importance cannot be overstated; effective feedback serves as a catalyst for growth, enabling both leaders and their teams to identify strengths, uncover areas for improvement, and tailor development efforts accordingly. This discussion explores the critical role of constructive feedback in fostering leadership and team growth, alongside strategies for giving and receiving feedback in a manner that promotes continuous improvement.

Constructive feedback, when delivered thoughtfully, has the power to illuminate paths for personal and professional development that might otherwise remain obscured. For leaders, receiving feedback provides an opportunity to gain insights into their leadership style, decision-making process, and interpersonal dynamics. It offers a unique lens through which the impact of their actions on team performance and morale can be viewed, encouraging a reflective approach to leadership.

Similarly, providing team members with regular, constructive feedback is essential for their development and engagement. It helps individuals understand how their contributions align with team goals and organizational objectives, reinforcing positive behaviors and guiding improvements where needed. The key to maximizing the impact of feedback lies in ensuring it is specific, actionable, and focused on behaviors rather than personal attributes.

Strategies for Giving Feedback

- Focus on Specific Behaviors: Avoid general comments and instead, focus on specific behaviors and their impact. This approach makes the feedback more actionable and less likely to be perceived as a personal critique.

- Be Timely: Provide feedback soon after the relevant behavior occurs to ensure clarity and relevance.

- Encourage Dialogue: Feedback should be a two-way conversation, where the recipient is encouraged to share their perspective and engage in a dialogue about potential paths for development.

- Balance Positive and Constructive Feedback: While it's important to address areas for improvement, recognizing and reinforcing what is working well is equally vital for motivation and morale.

Strategies for Receiving Feedback

- Approach with Openness: View feedback as a valuable opportunity for growth, approaching it with an open mind and a willingness to learn.

- Seek Clarification: If feedback is unclear or lacks specificity, ask for examples or further explanation to fully understand the issue and how you can address it.

- Reflect and Plan: Take time to reflect on the feedback received, considering how it aligns with your self-perception and development goals. Then, create an action plan to address areas for improvement.

- Follow Up: Engage in follow-up discussions to track progress on the areas highlighted in the feedback. This demonstrates your commitment to growth and allows for additional guidance and support.

Constructive feedback is a cornerstone of effective leadership and team performance. By embracing strategies that facilitate open, honest, and supportive feedback exchanges, leaders can foster an environment of trust, growth, and continuous improvement. This culture of feedback not only enhances individual and team performance but also contributes to the development of resilient, adaptable, and high-performing organizations.

Designing effective performance reviews is a critical component of leadership that impacts motivation, fairness, and alignment with organizational goals. Performance reviews, when done correctly, can transcend their traditional role of evaluation to become powerful tools for mentorship and development. This approach requires thoughtful preparation, clear communication, and a forward-looking perspective that focuses on growth as much as assessment.

At the heart of effective performance reviews is the principle of fairness and transparency. Reviews should be based on clear, predefined criteria that are understood by both the reviewer and the reviewee. This ensures that evaluations are objective and based on actual performance rather than subjective perceptions. Establishing these criteria in alignment with organizational goals ensures that individual performance is assessed not only on personal achievements but also on contributions to the broader objectives of the organization.

Another best practice involves the timing and frequency of reviews. Rather than relying solely on annual reviews, incorporating regular check-ins throughout the year can provide ongoing guidance and support. This approach allows for timely feedback and adjustments, ensuring that employees are consistently aligned with expectations and have the opportunity to correct course as needed.

The structure of the performance review meeting is also crucial. It should be a dialogue rather than a one-way communication, with opportunities for employees to express their views, concerns, and aspirations. Starting with highlights of achievements and strengths sets a positive tone, encouraging openness and engagement. Discussing areas for improvement should be framed constructively, focusing on future growth opportunities rather than dwelling on past shortcomings.

Using performance reviews as opportunities for mentorship and development involves shifting the focus from evaluation to empowerment. Leaders can achieve this by:

- Identifying specific areas for skill enhancement or professional growth and linking these to available resources, such as training programs or mentorship opportunities.

- Setting collaborative goals for the coming period, ensuring these are aligned with both the individual's career aspirations and the organization's strategic direction.

- Offering support in the form of regular follow-up meetings to discuss progress, challenges, and adjustments to the development plan.

Performance reviews should conclude with a clear action plan that outlines agreed-upon objectives, development activities, and timelines. This plan serves as a roadmap for the employee's growth and contribution to the organization, reinforcing the review's role as a developmental tool.

Designing effective performance reviews requires a balance of assessment and encouragement, focusing not only on where employees stand but also on where they can go. By structuring reviews to be motivational, fair, and development-oriented, leaders can enhance individual and team performance, foster a culture of continuous improvement, and drive organizational success.

Effective time management is essential for leaders seeking to maximize productivity, minimize stress, and achieve a balanced and fulfilling professional life. This examination delves into the principles and techniques of time management, offering insights into how leaders can more efficiently allocate their time, prioritize tasks, and leverage tools and technologies to enhance their effectiveness.

At the core of effective time management is the ability to distinguish between urgent and important tasks. This distinction allows leaders to focus on activities that contribute significantly to their long-term objectives, rather than being caught up in the immediacy of less consequential tasks. Techniques such as the Eisenhower Box or the Pareto Principle (80/20 rule) can guide leaders in identifying tasks that require their immediate attention and those that can be delegated, delayed, or deleted.

Another key aspect of time management is setting clear goals and objectives. By defining what needs to be accomplished over a day, a week, or a month, leaders can better organize their time and resources. Goal setting goes hand in hand with prioritization, ensuring that the most critical tasks are addressed first, and effort is allocated in alignment with strategic objectives.

Effective time management also involves creating structured schedules and routines. By planning their days and weeks in advance, leaders can allocate specific blocks of time to different activities, ensuring a balanced approach that includes time for strategic thinking, operational tasks, and personal development. Techniques such as time blocking or the Pomodoro Technique can help in creating focused work sessions, minimizing distractions, and enhancing productivity.

In addition to these techniques, a range of tools and technologies can aid leaders in managing their time more efficiently. Digital calendars, task management apps, and project management software offer platforms for scheduling, delegating, and tracking tasks. These tools not only help in organizing work but also provide insights into patterns of time use, enabling further optimization of time management strategies.

Effective time management also acknowledges the importance of breaks and downtime. Regular breaks throughout the day can improve concentration and creativity, preventing burnout and maintaining high levels of productivity over the long term. Similarly, ensuring adequate time for rest and leisure activities outside of work is crucial for maintaining overall well-being and performance.

Mastering the principles and techniques of time management enables leaders to navigate their responsibilities with greater ease and effectiveness. By prioritizing tasks, setting clear goals, establishing structured routines, and leveraging tools and technologies, leaders can enhance their productivity while reducing stress. This not only benefits their professional performance but also contributes to a more balanced and satisfying life.

Enhancing personal and team productivity is a constant pursuit for executives, driven by the need to achieve more in an increasingly demanding business environment. Practical tips and hacks can make a significant difference in how efficiently and effectively one can work, leading not only to improved outcomes but also to a better work-life balance. Among these strategies, delegation, limiting interruptions, and leveraging productivity software stand out as key approaches for executives looking to maximize their productivity and that of their teams.

Delegation is a critical skill for executives, enabling them to distribute tasks appropriately among team members. This not only ensures tasks are completed by those with the most relevant skills and experience but also frees up the executive's time to focus on strategic planning and decision-making. Effective delegation involves clearly communicating expectations, providing the necessary resources, and trusting team members to take ownership of their responsibilities. It's also essential for fostering a sense of accountability and development within the team.

Limiting interruptions is another crucial strategy for enhancing productivity. In today's connected world, executives are bombarded with emails, messages, and calls, which can fragment attention and reduce the quality of work. Strategies to limit these interruptions include setting specific times for checking emails and messages, holding regular "no-interruption" periods where focus can be directed entirely on critical tasks, and creating an environment that encourages deep work. Moreover, establishing clear communication channels and expectations around availability can help manage the demands of both team members and external stakeholders.

Leveraging productivity software is an increasingly popular approach for executives looking to streamline their workflows and enhance efficiency. Tools such as task management apps, digital calendars, and project management platforms can automate routine tasks, facilitate collaboration, and provide real-time insights into project progress. These tools can be particularly effective when integrated into the team's daily routines, ensuring everyone is aligned and can access the information they need to work effectively.

In addition to these strategies, it's important for executives to recognize the value of self-care in maintaining productivity. Regular exercise, adequate rest, and mindfulness practices can significantly impact one's ability to focus, make decisions, and lead effectively. Encouraging these practices within the team can also contribute to a healthier, more engaged, and productive workforce.

In essence, enhancing productivity as an executive involves a combination of strategic delegation, creating an environment that minimizes interruptions, and effectively using technology to streamline tasks. By adopting these practices, executives can not only improve their personal efficiency but also foster a culture of productivity and accountability within their teams, driving organizational success.

Cultivating a culture of continuous learning within an organization is pivotal in today's fast-paced and ever-evolving business landscape. Such a culture not only underscores the importance of personal and professional development but also positions the organization to maintain its competitive advantage and foster innovation. By embracing continuous learning, organizations can adapt to changes more swiftly, harness new opportunities, and address challenges with enhanced agility and creativity.

The importance of a learning culture cannot be overstated. It creates an environment where curiosity is encouraged, knowledge is shared, and growth is seen as a collective responsibility. In this setting, employees are more likely to feel valued and invested in, leading to higher engagement levels, job satisfaction, and retention rates. Moreover, a learning culture promotes the development of a more skilled and versatile workforce, capable of contributing to the organization's success in a variety of ways.

Continuous learning is integral to maintaining a competitive advantage. In industries where technological advancements and market dynamics can shift the landscape overnight, organizations that invest in learning are better equipped to stay ahead. This commitment to learning ensures that employees' skills remain relevant and that the organization continuously benefits from the latest knowledge and innovations. Furthermore, a learning culture fosters innovation by encouraging experimentation, critical thinking, and the exploration of new ideas. This openness to innovation can lead to breakthrough products, services, and processes that drive growth and differentiation in the market.

Leaders play a crucial role in promoting and modeling continuous learning within the organization. Strategies for leaders to foster a learning culture include:

1. Encouraging Exploration and Curiosity: Leaders can create an atmosphere where employees feel safe to explore new ideas, ask questions, and seek out learning opportunities. This might involve setting aside time for experimentation or personal development projects.

2. Providing Access to Learning Resources: Organizations can invest in a range of learning resources, such as online courses, workshops, and seminars. Making these resources readily available and relevant to employees' roles and career aspirations demonstrates a tangible commitment to their development.

3. Personal Example: Leaders should model continuous learning by engaging in their own professional development and sharing their learning experiences with the team. This sets a powerful example and signals that learning is valued at all levels of the organization.

4. Recognition and Reward: Acknowledging and rewarding efforts to learn and apply new knowledge can reinforce the importance of continuous improvement. This could be through formal recognition programs, opportunities for career advancement, or simply verbal acknowledgment in team meetings.

5. Creating Learning Communities: Encouraging the formation of learning groups or communities of practice within the organization can facilitate knowledge sharing and collaboration. These communities provide a forum for employees to learn from one another and collectively tackle challenges.

6. Integrating Learning into Performance Management: Making learning and development an integral part of performance

reviews and career planning conversations emphasizes its importance in career progression and organizational success.

Cultivating a culture of continuous learning is a strategic imperative for organizations aiming to navigate the complexities of the modern business environment successfully. By emphasizing the importance of ongoing development, fostering an environment that encourages exploration, and leading by example, leaders can build an organization that learns, adapts, and innovates continuously, driving sustained success and competitive advantage.

Integrating learning opportunities into everyday work processes is a powerful strategy to foster a culture of continuous improvement and innovation. Practical approaches such as mentoring, cross-training, and learning projects allow employees to develop new skills and knowledge within the flow of their regular duties, enhancing engagement and productivity. Additionally, leveraging technology and online resources can significantly facilitate continuous learning, making it more accessible and tailored to individual needs.

Mentoring relationships are a cornerstone of learning in the workplace, providing a structured yet flexible framework for knowledge transfer and professional development. Through mentoring, experienced employees can share insights, guidance, and feedback with less experienced colleagues, helping them navigate challenges and accelerate their growth. This one-on-one approach not only benefits the mentee but also offers mentors the opportunity to refine their leadership and communication skills.

Cross-training involves training team members in the roles and responsibilities of their colleagues. This practice not only ensures that the team can maintain productivity during absences but also encourages a deeper understanding of the organization's processes and challenges. Cross-training promotes empathy and collaboration among team members, as they gain appreciation for each other's contributions and challenges.

Learning projects offer a hands-on approach to development, allowing employees to apply new knowledge and skills to real-world challenges. By undertaking projects that stretch their capabilities, employees can explore new areas, innovate, and contribute to the organization's goals. These projects can be individual or team-based, encouraging both personal initiative and collaborative problem-solving.

Leveraging technology and online resources is another effective way to integrate learning into daily routines. Digital learning platforms, online courses, and virtual workshops provide flexible, on-demand access to a vast array of knowledge and expertise. Organizations can curate libraries of resources tailored to their industry and the specific development needs of their employees, encouraging self-directed learning.

Collaborative technologies such as forums, wikis, and social media platforms can also support learning by facilitating knowledge sharing and community building. These tools enable employees to ask questions, share insights, and collaborate on problem-solving, regardless of geographical location. To maximize the impact of these strategies, organizations should encourage a proactive approach to learning, where employees are empowered to identify their development needs and seek out relevant opportunities. Leaders can support this by setting aside time for learning activities, providing guidance on selecting resources, and recognizing and celebrating achievements in learning.

Incorporating learning into daily routines requires a commitment from both individuals and the organization. By prioritizing development, fostering an environment that supports learning, and leveraging technology, organizations can ensure that continuous learning becomes an integral part of how they operate, driving ongoing improvement, innovation, and success.

Creating a Comprehensive Performance Enhancement Plan involves a strategic amalgamation of feedback mechanisms, time management strategies, and continuous learning practices. This plan serves as a roadmap for both personal and team development, aiming to maximize performance, foster growth, and enhance productivity. By integrating these elements into a cohesive strategy, leaders can cultivate an environment that not only drives organizational success but also supports the professional and personal advancement of its members.

The first step in crafting this plan is to establish a foundation of effective feedback mechanisms. This involves setting up regular, structured feedback sessions that provide clear, actionable insights into individual and team performance. Such sessions should be designed to celebrate successes, identify areas for improvement, and set goals for future development. Incorporating a variety of feedback sources, including peer reviews, customer feedback, and self-assessment, can offer a well-rounded perspective on performance.

Time management strategies form the next pillar of the performance enhancement plan. This requires a careful analysis of current work processes to identify inefficiencies and time drains. Leaders can then implement practices such as prioritization of tasks based on their impact and urgency, delegation of appropriate responsibilities, and the adoption of tools and technologies that streamline workflows. Encouraging team members to develop personal time management plans can also help in aligning individual efforts with team and organizational goals.

The integration of continuous learning practices is essential to ensuring that the team remains adaptable and innovative. This can be achieved by identifying skill gaps and setting learning objectives that align with both individual career aspirations and organizational needs. Providing access to a variety of learning resources, such as online courses, workshops, and cross-training opportunities, enables team members to pursue their development goals. Furthermore, creating a culture that celebrates learning and encourages knowledge sharing can enhance the collective intelligence of the team.

To bring these elements together into a comprehensive performance enhancement plan, leaders should:

1. Define Clear Objectives: Start with a clear understanding of what you aim to achieve through the plan, both at an individual and team level.

2. Customize the Approach: Tailor the integration of feedback, time management, and learning practices to fit the unique needs and circumstances of the team.

3. Set Measurable Goals: Establish specific, measurable goals for each component of the plan, ensuring they contribute to the overarching objectives.

4. Create a Timeline: Develop a realistic timeline for implementing the plan, including milestones for assessing progress and making adjustments.

5. Foster Accountability and Support: Encourage team members to take ownership of their development, while providing the necessary support and resources to facilitate their growth.

6. Regularly Review and Adjust: Schedule periodic reviews of the plan to assess its effectiveness, celebrate achievements, and adjust strategies as needed based on feedback and changing conditions.

By thoughtfully integrating feedback mechanisms, time management strategies, and continuous learning practices, leaders can develop a dynamic and effective performance enhancement plan. This plan not only drives improved performance and productivity but also supports the ongoing development of the team, fostering a culture of excellence and continuous improvement.

Measuring and adjusting for success is a critical aspect of implementing performance enhancement strategies within any organization. This process involves tracking the impact of these strategies on leadership effectiveness and organizational outcomes, then making iterative improvements based on feedback and performance metrics. By systematically evaluating the results of performance enhancement efforts, leaders can refine their approaches to ensure they are meeting their goals and contributing positively to the organization's success.

To effectively measure the impact of performance enhancement strategies, leaders can employ a variety of methods. One approach is to use performance metrics that are aligned with the organization's strategic objectives. These metrics can include quantitative measures such as productivity levels, sales figures, customer satisfaction scores, and employee engagement rates. By comparing these metrics before and after the implementation of performance enhancement strategies, leaders can gauge the effectiveness of their efforts.

In addition to quantitative measures, qualitative feedback from employees, customers, and other stakeholders can provide valuable insights into the impact of performance enhancement strategies. This feedback can be gathered through surveys, interviews, and open forums, allowing leaders to understand the experiences and perceptions of those affected by their strategies.

Making iterative improvements based on feedback and performance metrics involves a continuous cycle of evaluation and adjustment. Leaders should regularly review the data and feedback collected to identify areas where performance enhancement strategies are working well and areas where adjustments are needed. This process might involve refining goals, trying new approaches, or discontinuing strategies that are not yielding the desired results.

Tips for making iterative improvements include being open to experimentation and learning from both successes and failures. Leaders should encourage a culture of continuous improvement within their organizations, where employees feel empowered to suggest changes and contribute to the refinement of performance enhancement strategies. Additionally, setting short-term milestones can help keep teams focused and motivated, while also providing opportunities for quick adjustments based on performance data.

Another important aspect of making iterative improvements is to communicate openly with the team about the findings from performance data and feedback. Sharing successes and challenges can foster a sense of ownership and engagement among employees, encouraging them to be active participants in the performance enhancement process.

Measuring and adjusting for success is an ongoing process that requires careful monitoring, open communication, and a willingness to make changes based on evidence. By employing a mix of quantitative and qualitative methods to track the impact of performance enhancement strategies, and by being responsive to feedback and performance metrics, leaders can continually refine their approaches to achieve optimal results for their teams and organizations.

In concluding this exploration of performance enhancement strategies for executive leaders, we have delved into the critical interplay between feedback mechanisms, effective time management, and the ethos of continuous learning. These strategies are not standalone solutions but are interconnected components that, when harmoniously integrated, can significantly elevate an executive's leadership performance and, by extension, the productivity and growth potential of their teams and organizations.

The essence of feedback lies in its power to illuminate both strengths and areas for improvement, providing a foundation upon which leaders can build and refine their approach to leadership. Coupled with effective time management, leaders can optimize their schedules and priorities, ensuring that their efforts and those of their team are aligned with the organization's strategic objectives. The commitment to continuous learning underscores the journey of leadership as one of ongoing development, where the pursuit of knowledge and adaptability to change are viewed as critical to navigating the complexities of the modern business landscape.

Readers are encouraged to actively engage with the exercises provided throughout this exploration to gain practical experience and deeper insights into enhancing their leadership performance. These exercises are designed to be reflective and actionable, offering leaders the opportunity to assess and apply these strategies within the context of their unique leadership challenges and organizational environments.

The journey of performance enhancement is ongoing, characterized by a cycle of assessment, action, and adaptation. It is incumbent upon leaders to foster an environment that is conducive to growth, productivity, and continuous improvement. This environment is one where feedback is welcomed and acted upon, where time is managed judiciously, and where learning is embraced as a lifelong endeavor. By embodying these principles, leaders not only elevate their performance but also inspire those around them to strive for excellence, contributing to the creation of organizations that are resilient, innovative, and primed for success.

Exercises for Chapter 6: Performance Enhancement Strategies

Exercise 14: Feedback Exercise with a Peer

This guided activity is designed to enhance your ability to give and receive feedback effectively, emphasizing the qualities of specificity, empathy, and actionability. Engaging in this exercise with a peer will not only improve your feedback skills but also offer insights into the impact of your communication style. Following the feedback exchange, reflection prompts will guide you to assess the experience and identify areas for improvement.

Step 1: Preparation

Select a Peer: Choose a colleague or professional peer willing to participate in this exercise. Ideally, select someone with whom you have worked closely enough to provide specific and meaningful feedback.

Set Guidelines: Agree on confidentiality and approach the exercise with openness and a commitment to constructive dialogue. Establish that feedback should be specific, empathetic, and actionable.

Step 2: Giving Feedback

1. Prepare Your Feedback: Think of a specific instance where your peer demonstrated notable performance or where there's room for improvement. Structure your feedback to include:

2. Specificity: Clearly describe the situation and behavior. Avoid generalizations.

3. Empathy: Express your feedback from a place of understanding and support. Consider your peer's perspective and frame your feedback in a way that respects their feelings.

4. Actionability: Suggest concrete steps or actions they can take to sustain their strengths or address areas for improvement.

5. Deliver Your Feedback: Share your feedback with your peer, adhering to the guidelines for specificity, empathy, and actionability. Be attentive to your tone and body language to ensure your message is received as intended.

Step 3: Receiving Feedback

- Listen Actively: As your peer provides feedback, focus on listening attentively without interrupting. Show openness and appreciation for their insights.

- Seek Clarification: If any part of the feedback is unclear, ask for specific examples to fully understand the perspective being shared.

- Reflect on the Feedback: Consider how the feedback aligns with your self-perception and what actions you can take in response.

Step 4: Reflection

After completing the feedback exchange, reflect on the experience using the following prompts.

Analyzing the Feedback Given:

- How well did I adhere to the principles of specificity, empathy, and actionability in my feedback?

- What challenges did I encounter in preparing and delivering feedback? How might I address these challenges in the future?

Evaluating the Feedback Received:

- How did the feedback I received align with my expectations and self-assessment?

- What steps can I take to act on the feedback and improve my performance?

Assessing the Overall Experience:

- What did I learn about the process of giving and receiving feedback?

- How can I apply these insights to improve my feedback delivery and receptiveness in the future?

This feedback exercise with a peer is an invaluable opportunity to develop your communication skills, deepen professional relationships, and foster a culture of continuous improvement. By actively engaging in this process and reflecting on your experiences, you can enhance your effectiveness as both a giver and receiver of feedback, contributing to your growth and the development of those around you.

Exercise 15: Implementing a Time Management Tool for a Week

This exercise encourages you to select and utilize a time management tool or technique for one week, with the aim of documenting your experience and noting any improvements in productivity. The purpose is to explore how different time management strategies can enhance your efficiency and effectiveness in both personal and professional settings. Following the week-long trial, a set of analytical questions will guide you through evaluating the tool or technique's effectiveness and determining its suitability for long-term integration into your routines.

Step 1: Selection of a Time Management Tool or Technique

Choose a time management tool or technique that you believe could positively impact your productivity. Options might include digital tools like scheduling apps or task managers, techniques such as the Pomodoro Technique or time blocking, or even traditional methods like to-do lists or prioritization matrices. Consider what aspect of your time management you're looking to improve and select a tool or technique accordingly.

Step 2: Implementation for One Week

- Initial Setup: If you're using a digital tool, spend some time setting it up to suit your needs. For techniques, outline how you plan to incorporate them into your daily routine.

- Daily Use: Dedicate the week to consistently using your chosen tool or technique. Be mindful of how it integrates with your tasks and activities, making adjustments as needed.

- Documentation: Keep a daily journal of your experience, noting any changes in your productivity, challenges faced, and overall satisfaction with the tool or technique.

Step 3: Analytical Evaluation

At the end of the week, review your documentation and reflect on your experience using the following questions:

Productivity Improvements:

- Did I notice an increase in my productivity? In what ways did the tool or technique contribute to this improvement?

- Were there specific tasks or types of work where the tool or technique was particularly effective?

Challenges and Adaptations:

- What challenges did I encounter while using this tool or technique? How did I address these challenges?

- Did I need to make any adaptations to the tool or technique to better suit my needs?

Ease of Integration:

- How easily was I able to integrate this tool or technique into my daily routine? Did it require significant changes to my usual workflow?

- How did the use of this tool or technique affect my stress levels or work-life balance?

Long-term Viability:

- Based on my experience, is this tool or technique something I can see myself using long-term?

- What potential benefits or drawbacks do I foresee in continuing to use this tool or technique?

Step 4: Decision on Long-term Integration

Based on your evaluation, decide whether the time management tool or technique you tested is something you want to integrate into your routines long-term. Consider whether the benefits outweigh any challenges faced and if it aligns with your overall productivity and time management goals.

This exercise is not just about testing a new tool or technique but about actively reflecting on and seeking ways to improve how you manage your time. By critically evaluating your experience, you can make informed decisions about how to best enhance your productivity and efficiency moving forward.

Exercises 16: Learning Opportunity Identification

This activity is tailored to assist leaders in identifying potential learning opportunities within their teams and planning actionable steps for their implementation. By engaging in this exercise, leaders will not only pinpoint areas for growth but also strategize on how to effectively cultivate a culture of continuous learning within their teams. The following discussion prompts are provided to encourage reflection on fostering a learning culture and navigating potential challenges that may arise.

Step 1: Identifying Learning Opportunities

1. Assess Team Skills and Knowledge: Begin by assessing the current skills and knowledge within your team. Identify any gaps or areas where improvement could enhance team performance or individual career growth.

2. Evaluate Business Goals and Objectives: Align the identified learning opportunities with the broader business goals and objectives. Determine how enhancing certain skills or knowledge areas could contribute to achieving these goals.

3. Consider Diverse Learning Formats: Recognize that learning can occur in various formats — from formal training and workshops to peer-to-peer learning and self-directed online courses.

Consider which formats might be most effective for addressing the identified gaps.

Step 2: Planning Actionable Steps

- Set Clear Learning Objectives: For each identified learning opportunity, set clear and achievable learning objectives. Ensure these objectives are aligned with both team needs and individual growth aspirations.

- Develop an Implementation Plan: Outline a plan for implementing the learning opportunities. This plan should include timelines, required resources, and how progress will be measured.

- Encourage Team Input and Engagement: Involve the team in the planning process. Seek their input on identified learning opportunities and preferred learning formats. This engagement can enhance buy-in and motivation.

Discussion Prompts

1. Fostering a Culture of Learning: Reflect on the steps that can be taken to foster a culture of continuous learning within your team.

2. Consider how leadership practices, team norms, and organizational policies can support or hinder this culture.

3. Navigating Challenges: Discuss potential challenges that may arise in implementing learning opportunities and fostering a learning culture. These might include time constraints, limited resources, or resistance to change. Consider strategies for overcoming these challenges.

4. Measuring Impact: Reflect on how the impact of learning opportunities can be measured both at the individual and team levels. Consider how improvements in performance, engagement, and innovation could be indicators of success.

5. Long-term Sustainability: Discuss strategies for ensuring the sustainability of a learning culture over the long term. Consider how learning can be integrated into regular team processes and how ongoing support for professional development can be provided.

By actively identifying learning opportunities and planning actionable steps for their implementation, leaders can significantly contribute to the professional development of their team members and the overall success of the organization. Engaging in reflective discussions on fostering a learning culture and navigating challenges further equips leaders to effectively support continuous growth and adaptability within their teams.

Part III: Advanced Coaching Techniques

In Part III, "Advanced Coaching Techniques," we delve into the nuanced and sophisticated aspects of coaching that enable leaders to not only meet but exceed the demands of today's dynamic and often volatile business environment. This section is designed to elevate the coaching conversation, focusing on transformative practices, executive presence and branding, and the complexities of global leadership. Through these advanced techniques, coaches can empower leaders to inspire change, foster innovation, and extend their influence across cultural and geographical boundaries.

Transformational coaching goes beyond conventional development frameworks, aiming to inspire profound change and personal growth in leaders. This chapter explores how coaches can facilitate transformation, guiding leaders to question their assumptions, envision new possibilities, and embrace change with resilience and optimism. By fostering a mindset geared toward innovation and creativity, coaches can help leaders become agents of change within their organizations, capable of navigating uncertainty with agility and confidence.

To embed these concepts, readers are encouraged to engage in vision statement development, articulating their aspirations and goals in a compelling and forward-looking manner. Additionally, a creative problem-solving workshop exercise will challenge readers to think outside the box, applying innovative solutions to complex scenarios.

Executive presence is an intangible yet critical aspect of effective leadership. This chapter addresses how leaders can cultivate a commanding presence that inspires confidence and respect.

Furthermore, it delves into the importance of personal branding for executive leaders, guiding them to articulate their unique value proposition and leverage it to build meaningful professional relationships.

Exercises include crafting a personal branding statement, helping readers to concisely communicate their strengths and leadership philosophy. A networking strategy plan exercise will equip readers with a structured approach to building and nurturing a professional network, enhancing their influence and opportunities for collaboration.

The global business landscape requires leaders to navigate cultural diversity with sensitivity and intelligence. This chapter introduces the concept of global leadership coaching, focusing on strategies for understanding and leveraging cultural differences to foster inclusive and effective leadership practices. It examines global trends and their impact on executive leadership, emphasizing the need for leaders to expand their influence on a global scale, while being mindful of local nuances and expectations.

A cultural intelligence quiz offers readers an opportunity to assess their cultural awareness and identify areas for improvement. Meanwhile, a global leadership challenge case study encourages the application of global leadership principles in a complex, multicultural context, enhancing readers' ability to lead with cultural competence and inclusivity.

Part III of this book provides a deep dive into the transformative aspects of leadership coaching, offering readers advanced techniques and exercises designed to challenge, inspire, and empower leaders to achieve their fullest potential. By embracing these advanced coaching techniques, leaders and coaches alike can navigate the complexities of the modern business world with greater impact and success.

Chapter 7: Transformational Executive Leadership Coaching

In the evolving landscape of executive leadership, the capacity to foster change, drive innovation, and instill resilience within organizations is more critical than ever. Transformational executive leadership coaching emerges as a pivotal force in this context, offering a pathway to profound, systemic change that transcends traditional coaching methods. This chapter introduces the concept of transformational coaching, elucidating its significance and differentiated approach in cultivating leaders and organizations equipped to navigate the complexities of the modern business world.

Transformational coaching is predicated on the belief that leadership effectiveness is deeply intertwined with personal growth and self-awareness. Unlike conventional coaching, which often focuses on specific skills or short-term objectives, transformational coaching delves into the foundational beliefs, values, and assumptions that underpin a leader's actions and decisions. This approach facilitates a deeper understanding of oneself and one's impact on others, paving the way for genuine, lasting change that can significantly influence organizational culture and performance.

At its core, transformational coaching aims to expand a leader's perspective, encouraging them to question established norms and explore new possibilities. This process of reflection and exploration is critical for fostering innovation and adaptability, enabling leaders to not only respond to challenges but also anticipate and shape the future. By focusing on deep, systemic change, transformational coaching helps leaders develop the agility and resilience needed to lead effectively in an environment marked by rapid change and uncertainty.

The significance of transformational coaching extends beyond individual leaders to impact the broader organization. Leaders who undergo transformational coaching often become catalysts for change, inspiring and empowering their teams to embrace new ideas, challenge the status quo, and strive for continuous improvement. This ripple effect can transform organizational culture, driving engagement, collaboration, and performance across all levels of the organization.

In this chapter, we will explore the principles and practices of transformational executive leadership coaching, including its theoretical underpinnings, key strategies, and the roles of both coach and coachee. Through real-world examples and practical insights, we aim to illuminate the transformative potential of this approach, offering leaders and organizations a roadmap to achieving lasting change and enduring success.

Transformational leadership stands at the forefront of inspiring change and driving transformation within organizations. This leadership approach is rooted in the capacity to envision a compelling future, inspire others to join in that vision, challenge existing paradigms, and empower individuals to exceed their own limitations. Central to transformational leadership is the idea that leaders can ignite significant, positive changes by embodying these key principles.

At the heart of transformational leadership lies the ability to articulate a clear and compelling vision. Leaders adept in this approach are not just focused on the present but are forward-thinking, crafting a vivid picture of what the future could hold. This vision serves as a guiding light, providing direction and purpose, and helping to align the efforts of the entire organization towards achieving common goals.

Inspiration is another cornerstone of transformational leadership. Through their passion, enthusiasm, and genuine belief in the vision, transformational leaders inspire their followers to embrace the journey ahead. This inspiration is contagious, fostering a shared sense of commitment and drive among team members to pursue the vision with vigor and determination.

Challenging the status quo is essential for transformation and growth. Transformational leaders are characterized by their willingness to question existing practices and beliefs, encouraging innovation and creative problem-solving. By fostering an environment where questioning and exploration are welcomed, these leaders pave the way for breakthroughs and advancements that can redefine industries.

Empowering others is a fundamental aspect of transformational leadership. Recognizing that the strength of an organization lies in its people, transformational leaders focus on developing and empowering their followers. This empowerment involves providing opportunities for growth, offering support and guidance, and encouraging autonomy. By investing in their followers' development, transformational leaders build a more capable, confident, and motivated workforce ready to take on challenges and contribute to the organization's success.

The principles of transformational leadership—vision, inspiration, challenging the status quo, and empowering others—form a powerful framework for driving change and fostering an environment of continuous improvement and innovation. Leaders who embrace these principles can inspire their teams to achieve extraordinary results, transforming not just their organizations but also the individuals within them. Through transformational leadership, the potential for positive change becomes boundless, with far-reaching impacts that extend beyond the immediate organizational context.

Coaches play a pivotal role in facilitating transformation, acting as catalysts that guide individuals through the process of self-discovery, reflection, and the exploration of new possibilities. By fostering an environment of trust and openness, coaches can encourage leaders and individuals to delve into the depths of their beliefs, values, and behaviors, uncovering insights that can lead to profound personal and professional growth.

One of the key ways coaches facilitate transformation is by encouraging self-awareness. Through thoughtful questioning and active listening, coaches help individuals gain a deeper understanding of their own motivations, emotional responses, and the impact of their actions on others. This heightened self-awareness is the foundation for transformation, as it enables individuals to recognize patterns that may be limiting their effectiveness and to identify strengths they can leverage more fully.

Reflection is another critical aspect of the transformational process that coaches support. Coaches provide the space and structure for individuals to reflect on their experiences, challenges, and successes. This reflective process allows individuals to process learning, integrate new insights, and consider how they can apply their understanding in practical ways. By guiding individuals to reflect on their journey, coaches help to embed learning and ensure that insights lead to actionable change.

- Coaches encourage the exploration of new possibilities. They challenge individuals to step out of their comfort zones, question assumptions, and consider alternative perspectives. This exploration is vital for transformation, as it opens up new pathways for thinking and acting. Coaches support individuals in envisioning different futures and experimenting with new behaviors, fostering innovation and adaptability.

- Coaches also play a significant role in building resilience and confidence, equipping individuals to navigate the uncertainties and setbacks that often accompany transformational efforts. By providing encouragement, feedback, and support, coaches help individuals to maintain momentum and stay committed to their growth, even when faced with challenges.

- Coaches can influence the broader organizational culture by modeling transformational behaviors and practices. By demonstrating openness, curiosity, and a commitment to continuous learning, coaches can inspire others within the organization to embrace these values, further embedding a culture of transformation.

In summary, executive coaches are instrumental in facilitating transformation by promoting self-awareness, guiding reflection, encouraging the exploration of new possibilities, and supporting resilience and confidence. Through their partnership, coaches help individuals and organizations unlock their potential, navigate change more effectively, and achieve lasting growth and success.

Inspiring leaders to embrace change requires a nuanced understanding of human behavior and motivation. Effective change agents employ a variety of techniques and approaches to influence leaders' perceptions and attitudes towards change. Among these strategies, storytelling, modeling behavior, and leveraging intrinsic motivation stand out as particularly impactful.

Storytelling is a powerful tool for inspiring change. By sharing compelling narratives about individuals or organizations that have successfully navigated change, leaders can visualize the potential outcomes and benefits of embracing new ways of thinking and acting. Stories that highlight overcoming challenges, innovative problem-solving, and the positive impact of change on people's lives resonate deeply, creating an emotional connection to the desired transformation. This emotional engagement can break down resistance and inspire leaders to embark on their own change journeys.

Modeling behavior is another critical strategy. Leaders look to their peers and superiors for cues on how to behave, especially in times of uncertainty. When change agents consistently demonstrate the behaviors and attitudes they advocate for, they provide a living example of the change in action. This includes showing adaptability, resilience, openness to learning, and a positive outlook on the challenges and opportunities that change presents. By modeling these behaviors, change agents can inspire leaders to mirror these actions, fostering a culture where change is embraced and celebrated.

Leveraging intrinsic motivation taps into the internal drivers that compel leaders to act. Understanding what motivates leaders at a deep level—such as the desire for mastery, autonomy, purpose, and connection—allows change agents to frame change initiatives in ways that align with these intrinsic motivators. For instance, presenting change as an opportunity for leaders to develop new skills (mastery), exercise greater creativity and independence in their roles (autonomy), contribute to meaningful organizational goals (purpose), or strengthen team collaboration (connection) can significantly enhance their engagement and commitment to change.

In addition to these strategies, fostering an environment that supports risk-taking and experimentation is crucial for inspiring change. Leaders are more likely to embrace change when they feel safe to try new approaches, learn from failures, and iterate on their ideas. Creating a culture that values learning and growth over perfection and encourages open dialogue about the change process can demystify change and make it more accessible and appealing.

Inspiring leaders to embrace change is a multifaceted process that requires a combination of storytelling, modeling behavior, leveraging intrinsic motivation, and creating a supportive environment. By employing these strategies, change agents can effectively influence leaders' attitudes and behaviors, paving the way for meaningful and lasting transformation within organizations.

Fostering a creative mindset among leaders is crucial in today's rapidly changing business environment, where innovation and adaptability are key drivers of success. Executive coaches play a significant role in encouraging leaders to embrace creativity, guiding them to see beyond conventional strategies and develop new solutions to complex challenges. Here are insights into how coaches can cultivate a culture of creativity and innovation within leaders.

1. Encourage Curiosity and Exploration: Coaches can stimulate a leader's curiosity by prompting them to ask open-ended questions about their business, industry, and the broader world. Encouraging leaders to explore diverse fields of knowledge and seek inspiration outside their comfort zones can spark creative ideas and innovative solutions.

2. Create a Safe Space for Experimentation: One of the critical roles of an executive coach is to create a judgment-free environment where leaders feel safe to experiment with new ideas without fear of failure. Coaches can emphasize the value of experimentation and learning from mistakes as essential components of the creative process.

3. Challenge Assumptions: Coaches can encourage leaders to challenge the assumptions underlying their decision-making processes and business models. By questioning these assumptions, leaders can uncover alternative approaches and perspectives, opening up new possibilities for innovation.

4. Promote Divergent Thinking: Executive coaches can introduce exercises that promote divergent thinking, encouraging leaders to generate multiple solutions to a given problem. Techniques such as brainstorming, mind mapping, or scenario planning can help leaders break free from linear thinking patterns and embrace a more expansive view of potential strategies.

5. Leverage Storytelling: Through storytelling, coaches can illustrate how creativity has led to breakthrough innovations in various industries. Sharing stories of successful innovators and creative problem-solvers can inspire leaders to pursue their creative ventures.

6. Model a Creative Mindset: Coaches themselves can model a creative mindset by demonstrating flexibility in their coaching

approach, adapting methods to suit the leader's unique context, and bringing fresh perspectives to each session. This modeling can subtly encourage leaders to adopt similar behaviors in their leadership style.

7. Encourage Reflective Practice: Coaches can guide leaders in reflective practices that deepen their understanding of where creativity comes from and how it can be stifled or encouraged. Reflecting on past experiences of creativity and innovation can help leaders identify what conditions foster their best ideas.

8. Build Creative Confidence: By providing positive reinforcement and highlighting instances where a leader's creative approach has led to successful outcomes, coaches can build a leader's confidence in their creative abilities. Over time, this confidence encourages leaders to take more creative risks and champion innovation within their teams.

9. Facilitate Cross-Pollination of Ideas: Executive coaches can encourage leaders to facilitate the exchange of ideas within their organizations, creating cross-functional teams or organizing ideation sessions that bring together diverse perspectives. This cross-pollination can lead to unexpected insights and innovative solutions.

By employing these strategies, executive coaches can effectively encourage leaders to adopt a mindset that values creativity and innovation. This shift not only enhances the leader's capacity to drive change and innovation but also contributes to creating a culture that embraces creativity as a core organizational value.

Tools and methodologies that enhance creative problem-solving offer a structured yet flexible approach to tackling challenges in innovative ways. Among these, design thinking and brainstorming techniques stand out for their ability to facilitate the generation of novel solutions and encourage a user-centric perspective in problem-solving.

Design thinking is a human-centered approach to innovation that integrates the needs of people, the possibilities of technology, and the requirements for business success. It involves five phases: empathize, define, ideate, prototype, and test. This process encourages leaders and teams to immerse themselves in the user's experience, clearly define the problem, generate a wide array of solutions, create prototypes, and then test these solutions with real users. By fostering empathy and focusing on the end user's needs, design thinking helps teams break free from traditional constraints and explore a broader range of possibilities.

Brainstorming techniques are another critical tool in the creative problem-solving toolkit. The classic brainstorming approach involves gathering a group and encouraging the free flow of ideas without immediate judgment or analysis. This technique aims to produce a high volume of ideas in a short period, fostering creative thinking and group dynamics. Variations of brainstorming, such as brainwriting, where ideas are written down before being shared, or role-storming, where participants assume different personas, can provide fresh perspectives and stimulate innovative thinking.

Other tools and techniques that facilitate creative thinking include:

- SCAMPER: An acronym for Substitute, Combine, Adapt, Modify, Put to another use, Eliminate, and Reverse, SCAMPER is a checklist-based tool that prompts individuals to think about a product, service, or process in different ways.

- Mind Mapping: This tool helps in visually organizing information, making it easier to see relationships between ideas and explore new connections. Mind mapping can be particularly useful in the ideation phase to expand on initial thoughts and generate deeper insights.

- Six Thinking Hats: Developed by Edward de Bono, this technique encourages teams to look at problems from six distinct perspectives (emotional, informational, logical negative, logical positive, creative, and management) to explore all aspects of a situation before making a decision.

- Analogical Thinking: This involves drawing parallels between unrelated domains or industries to find innovative solutions to existing problems. By looking at how challenges are addressed in different contexts, teams can uncover unique approaches applicable to their situation.

Integrating these tools and techniques into the problem-solving process can significantly enhance an organization's capacity for creative thinking. By fostering an environment that values and practices these methodologies, leaders can encourage teams to approach challenges with a fresh perspective, explore a wide range of potential solutions, and ultimately, drive innovation within the organization.

Creating an environment that supports innovation is essential for organizations looking to thrive in the fast-paced, ever-changing business landscape. This requires a strategic approach to culture-building, where experimentation is encouraged, failure is tolerated as a learning opportunity, and novel solutions are celebrated. Here are strategies to cultivate such an environment:

Establish a clear vision for innovation that aligns with the organization's overall objectives. Leaders should communicate this vision effectively, ensuring that all team members understand the importance of innovation to the organization's success and how they can contribute. This shared vision serves as a guiding light, motivating individuals to seek out creative solutions and new opportunities.

Foster a culture of experimentation by providing employees with the resources and autonomy they need to explore new ideas. This might involve allocating time for employees to work on innovation projects, providing access to the tools and technologies necessary for experimentation, or setting up dedicated innovation labs or spaces where ideas can be developed and tested.

Normalize failure and reframe it as a learning opportunity. To truly support innovation, organizations must move away from a fear of failure and instead embrace it as an integral part of the creative process. Leaders can model this attitude by openly discussing their own failures and the lessons learned, as well as by celebrating the risks taken by teams, regardless of the outcome.

Encourage cross-functional collaboration to bring together diverse perspectives and expertise. Innovation often occurs at the intersection of different fields and ideas, so facilitating collaboration across departments can spark creative solutions that might not emerge within siloed teams. This can be achieved through cross-functional projects, innovation workshops, or regular idea-sharing sessions.

Provide recognition and rewards for innovative efforts and achievements. Celebrating both the process and the outcomes of innovation reinforces its value to the organization. Recognition can take many forms, from formal awards and promotions to simple acknowledgments in team meetings. Rewards should not only be reserved for successful innovations but also for noteworthy attempts that contribute to the organization's learning and growth.

Implement mechanisms for capturing and evaluating ideas from all levels of the organization. An open-door policy for idea submission, regular innovation challenges, or digital platforms for idea sharing can ensure that valuable insights from employees are heard and considered. It's important to provide feedback on submitted ideas, further encouraging engagement and participation.

Invest in ongoing learning and development to equip employees with the skills and knowledge needed to innovate. This might include training in creative problem-solving techniques, exposure to emerging technologies, or opportunities to attend industry conferences. A workforce that is continually learning is more likely to generate fresh ideas and view challenges through a new lens.

Building an environment that supports innovation requires a multifaceted approach centered on fostering experimentation, normalizing failure, and celebrating novel solutions. By implementing these strategies, leaders can cultivate a culture that not only encourages innovation but also empowers employees to actively contribute to the organization's creative and competitive edge.

Leading through change and uncertainty presents a unique set of challenges and opportunities for leaders. In today's fast-paced business environment, change is a constant, driven by technological advancements, market dynamics, and global events. Navigating the complexities of change requires a blend of strategic foresight, adaptability, and resilience. Understanding both the hurdles and the potential benefits of change can equip leaders to guide their organizations more effectively through periods of uncertainty.

Challenges of change often stem from resistance within the organization. This resistance can be due to fear of the unknown, loss of control, or concern over potential impacts on roles and routines. Additionally, rapid or significant change can lead to confusion and ambiguity, making it difficult for teams to maintain focus and productivity. For leaders, the challenge lies in managing these emotional and operational impacts while steering the organization towards its new direction.

Change also presents opportunities for growth and innovation. It can serve as a catalyst for reevaluating outdated processes and assumptions, encouraging creativity and new ways of thinking. Change can also strengthen an organization by building resilience and flexibility, qualities that are invaluable in an unpredictable business landscape.

To effectively navigate through uncertainty, leaders should adopt several key approaches:

- Communicate Clearly and Transparently: Open, honest communication is crucial during times of change. Leaders should strive to communicate the reasons behind the change, the expected outcomes, and how it will impact individuals and teams. Providing regular updates and being available to answer questions can help alleviate concerns and build trust.

- Foster a Culture of Flexibility and Adaptability: Encouraging a mindset of flexibility and adaptability among team members can make navigating change easier. This includes being open to new ideas, willing to abandon old ways of working, and able to adjust plans as circumstances evolve.

- Empower and Support Your Team: Empowering team members by involving them in the change process and supporting them through transitions can enhance buy-in and reduce resistance. Providing resources, training, and emotional support can help teams adjust more quickly and effectively.

- Lead by Example: Leaders should model the behaviors they wish to see in their teams. Demonstrating resilience, optimism, and a commitment to navigating the change successfully can inspire and motivate others.

- Leverage Change Management Tools and Frameworks: Utilizing established change management methodologies can provide a structured approach to implementing change. Tools such as stakeholder analysis, impact assessments, and communication plans can help manage the process more effectively.

- Encourage Innovation and Creativity: Change often requires innovative solutions. Leaders should encourage creativity and experimentation, creating an environment where new ideas are welcomed and explored.

- Build Resilience: Preparing for future uncertainties by building organizational resilience is key. This can involve diversifying products or services, investing in employee development, and creating flexible operational strategies.

In navigating the complexities of change, leaders must balance the need to move forward with the need to support and involve their teams. By viewing change as an opportunity for growth and by employing strategies to manage its challenges, leaders can guide their organizations through uncertainty with confidence and clarity. This approach not only ensures the organization's survival but also positions it to thrive in a changing world.

Building resilience and adaptability in leaders is essential for ensuring they can effectively navigate through challenges, recover from setbacks, and capitalize on new opportunities. These qualities are the bedrock upon which leaders can maintain focus and drive, even as conditions around them shift. To cultivate resilience and adaptability, leaders are encouraged to develop a growth mindset, seeing challenges as opportunities for learning rather than barriers. This mindset shift is crucial for fostering a positive approach to problem-solving and continuous improvement.

Accepting change as an inevitable part of the business landscape is another key strategy. By embracing change, leaders can move from attempting to avoid it to mastering the art of navigating through it. This involves enhancing emotional intelligence, which allows leaders to manage their emotions and those of their team effectively during times of stress, thereby contributing to a resilient and adaptable leadership style.

Building and maintaining a supportive network of colleagues, mentors, and peers provides leaders with a foundation of advice, encouragement, and diverse perspectives that are invaluable during challenging times. Alongside this, prioritizing self-care and well-being is crucial; leaders need to sustain their physical and mental health to maintain energy and focus, which are essential for resilience.

Engaging in scenario and contingency planning prepares leaders for a range of potential challenges, making unexpected changes less daunting and enhancing adaptability. Furthermore, promoting a reflective practice where leaders regularly consider their experiences, decisions, and their outcomes fosters a learning environment that encourages adaptation and growth.

Creating a culture that values learning and innovation encourages leaders to experiment and take calculated risks, enhancing their adaptability. Strengthening problem-solving skills through training and practice ensures leaders are well-equipped to identify issues and implement effective solutions swiftly.

An organizational culture that normalizes and de-stigmatizes failure is also vital. Viewing setbacks as part of the learning process rather than defeats enables leaders to approach challenges with resilience, seeing them as opportunities for growth rather than reasons for despair.

By integrating these strategies into their leadership approach, leaders can build the resilience and adaptability needed to thrive in today's ever-changing business environment. These traits not only empower leaders to withstand pressures but also inspire their teams, fostering a culture of resilience and adaptability across the organization.

Communicating through change is a critical aspect of leadership, particularly during periods of transition where uncertainty can lead to resistance and misalignment within the organization. Best practices for transparent and effective communication involve clarity, empathy, and consistency, which together ensure that all team members are on the same page and feel supported throughout the change process.

Clarity is paramount in change communication. Leaders must articulate the reasons behind the change, the expected outcomes, and the steps involved in the transition process. Clear communication helps demystify the change, reducing anxiety and speculation among team members. It's essential to outline not only what is changing but also what will remain the same, providing a sense of stability and continuity amidst the transition.

Empathy plays a significant role in effective communication during change. Leaders should acknowledge the emotions and concerns that change may evoke among team members. Demonstrating understanding and compassion towards these feelings can build trust and open lines of communication, making it easier to address concerns and mitigate resistance. Empathetic communication also involves actively listening to feedback and questions from team members, showing that their input is valued and considered in the change process.

Consistency in messaging is critical to avoid confusion and ensure alignment across the organization. Leaders should coordinate to deliver consistent information through all communication channels, whether in meetings, emails, or informal conversations. Repeating key messages and reinforcing the vision and benefits of the change can help embed the reasons for the transition in the team's consciousness, fostering a shared understanding and commitment to the change.

Involving team members in the change process can further enhance communication effectiveness. By engaging team members in discussions about the change, soliciting their ideas for implementation, and involving them in decision-making where appropriate, leaders can foster a sense of ownership and participation among the team. This inclusive approach can reduce resistance and build enthusiasm for the change.

Providing regular updates is another best practice in communicating through change. Keeping team members informed about progress, challenges, and next steps maintains transparency and keeps the momentum of the change process. It also provides opportunities for celebrating milestones and successes, reinforcing the value of the change and the team's efforts.

Preparing for and addressing resistance directly is an important aspect of communication during change. Leaders should anticipate potential sources of resistance and plan their communication strategies accordingly. Addressing concerns head-on, providing clear rationales, and demonstrating how feedback has been incorporated into the change process can help dissipate resistance and build support for the transition.

By adhering to these best practices—emphasizing clarity, empathy, consistency, involvement, regular updates, and direct addressing of resistance—leaders can navigate their teams through change with transparent and effective communication. This approach not only ensures alignment and reduces resistance but also strengthens the organization's capacity to adapt and thrive in the face of change.

Integrating transformational coaching practices into a comprehensive plan is an intricate process that aligns closely with both the individual leader's developmental needs and the overarching goals of their organization. This approach to coaching transcends mere performance improvement, delving into the deeper layers of a leader's psyche, including their core values, beliefs, and the foundational principles that guide their decision-making. Such a deep, introspective journey sets the stage for meaningful and enduring change, impacting not just the individual leader but also the broader organizational culture and performance metrics.

The process begins with a thorough assessment of the leader's existing competencies, behaviors, and overall performance, incorporating feedback from a wide range of sources including peers, subordinates, and superiors, alongside various self-assessment tools. This initial step aims to identify the leader's strengths as well as pinpoint areas in need of development, ensuring these are in harmony with the strategic objectives of the organization.

Following this assessment, the next phase involves defining a clear and compelling vision for the leader's growth, both personally and professionally. This vision should resonate with the leader's personal values and aspirations while also aligning with the needs and goals of the organization. A well-articulated vision serves as a motivational beacon throughout the coaching journey, encouraging the leader to engage deeply with the process of change.

Objectives for the coaching plan should be set with specificity and measurability in mind, crafted to challenge the leader yet remain within the realm of achievability. These objectives act as signposts along the coaching journey, offering a clear roadmap for progress and a means to measure success.

Choosing the right transformational coaching techniques is crucial, and these should be tailored to fit the unique style and preferences of the leader, as well as the specific objectives laid out in the coaching plan. Techniques might range from reflective questioning to enhance self-awareness, to role-playing for behavioral practice, to guided visualization techniques that reinforce the leader's vision for change.

An action plan detailing the steps required to achieve the set objectives is essential, including timelines, milestones, and necessary resources. This plan should be dynamic, with regular reviews to ensure its continued relevance and effectiveness in light of the leader's growth and any shifts within the organizational context.

Creating a supportive organizational environment is paramount, one that provides the necessary resources for learning and opportunities for the leader to apply new skills. This environment should also promote a culture that values feedback, continuous improvement, and recognizes the efforts and achievements made on the journey.

Monitoring progress is an ongoing requirement, utilizing feedback sessions, performance reviews, and other relevant metrics to gauge advancement towards objectives. This reflective process allows for the celebration of milestones, identification of any hurdles, and the necessary recalibration of the coaching plan to meet evolving needs.
Through this detailed and reflective approach, transformational coaching practices are seamlessly woven into a cohesive plan that

not only fosters the leader's personal and professional growth but also aligns with and propels the organization's strategic ambitions forward. This holistic process underscores the dynamic nature of leadership development, emphasizing flexibility, commitment, and a collaborative spirit between the coach, the leader, and the organization at large.

Measuring the impact of transformational coaching interventions is essential for understanding their influence on leadership behavior and organizational performance. This assessment process starts by establishing baseline measurements before the coaching begins, capturing the leader's initial performance levels and the organization's key performance indicators (KPIs). Such baselines enable a comparison of pre- and post-coaching states, offering a clear picture of progress.

The effectiveness of transformational coaching hinges on setting clear, measurable goals that align with both individual growth and organizational objectives. These goals form the basis for evaluating the coaching intervention, focusing the assessment on specific improvement areas. Utilizing both pre- and post-coaching assessments provides tangible evidence of change, allowing for a direct comparison of leadership behaviors and competencies before and after the coaching period.

Collecting feedback from various stakeholders, including the coachee, their peers, direct reports, and supervisors, enriches the evaluation process. This multi-source feedback sheds light on changes in the leader's approach, communication style, and overall effectiveness. Additionally, monitoring shifts in organizational performance indicators linked to the coaching goals can reveal the broader impact of the coaching on the organization.

Assessing the return on investment (ROI) of transformational coaching by comparing the intervention's costs against the financial gains from performance improvements offers a quantitative measure of its value. While some benefits of coaching, such as enhanced self-awareness and stronger team relationships, may be more challenging to quantify, they are no less significant. These qualitative changes, often captured through reflective journals or narrative feedback, provide insights into the nuanced ways coaching fosters growth.

A long-term perspective is crucial for fully appreciating the impact of transformational coaching. Longitudinal tracking of the leader's development and the sustained improvement within the organization acknowledges that the true benefits of coaching unfold over time. This comprehensive approach to assessment, combining quantitative and qualitative methods, not only validates the effectiveness of transformational coaching but also informs ongoing development strategies. It ensures that leaders and organizations are well-positioned to continue evolving in response to the dynamic demands of the business world.

In exploring the transformative power of executive leadership coaching, we've delved into its critical role in inspiring change, fostering innovation, and leading effectively through uncertainty. This journey has highlighted how coaching transcends conventional development methods, instead facilitating deep, systemic change that not only enhances individual leadership capabilities but also propels organizations forward. Through the lens of transformational coaching, leaders are encouraged to embrace self-awareness, challenge existing paradigms, and cultivate a culture of continuous learning and adaptability.

The essence of transformational coaching lies in its ability to inspire profound change—equipping leaders with the tools and insights needed to navigate the complexities of the modern business environment. By focusing on personal growth and organizational objectives, transformational coaching supports leaders in developing the resilience, creativity, and strategic vision required to drive lasting success.

Coaches and leaders alike are encouraged to embrace transformational practices as a means to unlock significant personal and organizational growth. This approach not only addresses immediate leadership challenges but also prepares leaders to anticipate future trends and lead with confidence and agility. Embracing transformational coaching practices represents a commitment to not just incremental improvements, but to achieving a level of excellence that can significantly impact an organization's trajectory.

As we conclude this exploration, it's clear that the journey of transformational leadership is ongoing, marked by a relentless pursuit of excellence and a continuous process of development. Transformational coaching is not a one-time intervention but a sustained partnership that evolves alongside the leader and the organization. The journey is characterized by moments of insight, challenge, and breakthrough, each contributing to the leader's ability to effect meaningful change.

In embracing the principles of transformational coaching, leaders and coaches commit to a path of relentless growth and innovation. This journey requires courage, openness to change, and a steadfast commitment to developing not just as a leader but as a person. The rewards of this journey extend beyond individual achievements, influencing the lives of others and shaping the future of organizations and communities.

Transformational coaching offers more than just a pathway to improved leadership effectiveness; it offers a vision for what leadership can be in the 21st century—dynamic, empathetic, and transformative. As we continue to navigate the challenges and opportunities of an ever-changing world, the principles of transformational coaching remain a beacon, guiding leaders towards a future where they can thrive and inspire others to do the same.

Exercises for Chapter 7: Transformational Executive Leadership Coaching

Exercise 17: Vision Statement Development

This exercise is a structured activity designed to guide leaders through the process of articulating a compelling vision statement. This statement should reflect their aspirations for personal change, growth, and the legacy they aim to create. Crafting a vision statement is a deeply reflective exercise, encouraging leaders to consider their core values, the impact they wish to have, and how they envision their future. Here is a step-by-step guide to developing your vision statement:

Step 1: Reflect on Personal Values

Begin by considering the values that are most important to you both personally and professionally. These values serve as the foundation of your vision statement, guiding your actions and decisions. Ask yourself:

- What principles guide my leadership style?

- Which values are non-negotiable in my work and life?

Step 2: Envision the Desired Impact

Think about the impact you want to have through your leadership. This could relate to your team, organization, community, or even on a broader scale. Consider:

- What positive changes do I want to instigate?

- How do I want to influence those around me?

Step 3: Contemplate the Legacy

Reflect on the legacy you wish to leave behind. This is about the long-term effects of your leadership and how you want to be remembered. Ask yourself:

- What do I want people to say about my leadership in the future?

- How can I make a lasting difference?

Step 4: Draft Your Vision Statement

Using your reflections, start drafting a vision statement that encapsulates your values, desired impact, and the legacy you aim to create. Keep it concise and inspiring—a statement that you can easily recall and that motivates you to action.

Step 5: Refine and Finalize

Review your draft and refine it. Ensure it truly reflects your aspirations and serves as a guiding light for your leadership journey. You may want to share it with trusted peers or mentors for feedback.

Reflection Prompts:

- How does this vision statement inspire me to grow as a leader?

- In what ways can I align my daily actions and decisions with this vision?

- What are the first steps I can take to start realizing this vision?

Developing a vision statement is more than an exercise; it's a commitment to yourself and your future. It requires deep introspection and honesty, but the result is a clear, powerful declaration of your leadership intentions and aspirations. This vision statement becomes a touchstone for decision-making and a source of inspiration during challenging times, guiding you towards the lasting impact and legacy you wish to achieve.

Exercise 18: Creative Problem-Solving Workshop

Welcome to an interactive session designed to immerse leaders in complex challenges, guiding them through a structured process of creative problem-solving. The goal is to not only find innovative solutions but also reflect on the creative process itself and explore ways to cultivate a culture of innovation within their teams. Here's how to structure this workshop:

Workshop Setup

1. Select Complex Challenges: Begin by choosing real-world challenges that your organization or industry is facing. These should be complex enough to require creative thinking and should not have straightforward solutions.

2. Divide into Small Groups: Participants should be divided into small groups to encourage collaboration and diverse perspectives. Each group is assigned one of the complex challenges to work on.

3. Introduce Creative Problem-Solving Frameworks: Before diving into the challenges, introduce participants to various creative problem-solving frameworks such as Design Thinking, the Six Thinking Hats, or SCAMPER. Provide a brief overview of how each framework can be used to approach problems creatively.

Guided Problem-Solving Process

1. Empathize and Define: Encourage groups to first empathize with the stakeholders affected by the challenge and then clearly define the problem they are trying to solve. This step ensures that the solutions developed are user-centric and address the root cause of the issue.

2. Ideate: Facilitate an ideation phase where participants brainstorm as many solutions as possible without judgment.

Encourage wild ideas and build on each other's thoughts to foster creativity.

3. Prototype: Have each group select one or two ideas to develop further into prototypes. These can be simple models or diagrams that convey how the solution would work.

4. Test and Iterate: Groups present their prototypes to the wider workshop for feedback. Encourage constructive criticism and suggestions for improvement, allowing groups to iterate on their designs.

Reflection and Discussion

Reflect on the Creative Process: After the workshop, guide participants in a reflection on the creative process. Discuss what strategies were most effective in generating innovative solutions and what challenges were encountered.

Innovative Solutions in Teams: Facilitate a discussion on how the creative problem-solving methods experienced in the workshop can be fostered within their own teams. Consider questions like:

- How can we create an environment that encourages creative thinking?

- What changes can we make to our team processes to incorporate regular brainstorming and ideation?

- How can we ensure that all team members feel empowered to contribute innovative ideas?

Action Planning: Encourage leaders to develop an action plan for integrating creative problem-solving techniques into their team's routine. This might involve regular creative workshops, setting aside time for brainstorming sessions, or implementing a system for capturing and evaluating innovative ideas.

The Creative Problem-Solving Workshop is more than just an exercise in finding solutions; it's an opportunity for leaders to experience firsthand the power of creativity and collaboration. By reflecting on the process and discussing ways to apply these strategies within their teams, leaders can lay the groundwork for a culture that not only values but thrives on innovation.

Exercise 19: Scenario Planning for Leaders

Scenario Planning is designed to engage leaders in the process of preparing for various future states, enhancing their strategic foresight and ability to navigate uncertainty. This exercise not only helps leaders anticipate changes and challenges but also underscores the importance of flexibility, preparedness, and continuous learning in effective leadership. Here's how to conduct this exercise:

Scenario Planning Process:

1. Introduction to Scenario Planning: Begin by introducing the concept of scenario planning as a strategic tool used to envision different future states based on varying factors or decisions. Emphasize its value in enhancing adaptability and strategic thinking.

2. Identify Key Factors: Leaders are first asked to identify key factors that could impact their organization in the future. These factors might include technological advancements, market trends, regulatory changes, or geopolitical events. Encourage leaders to consider both internal and external factors.

3. Develop Scenarios: Based on the identified factors, guide leaders in developing a range of plausible scenarios. Each scenario should represent a distinct future state, considering different combinations of the identified factors and their potential impact on the organization.

4. Analyze Scenarios: For each scenario, leaders analyze potential challenges and opportunities that could arise. They are tasked with considering how their organization would need to adapt to thrive in each of these future states. This analysis should cover strategic, operational, and leadership implications.

5. Strategize Responses: Leaders then develop strategic responses for each scenario. This involves outlining action

plans, resource allocations, and changes in organizational processes or structures that would be necessary to navigate each future state successfully.

6. Prepare for Implementation: Finally, leaders consider how to integrate insights from scenario planning into their current strategic planning processes. This might involve setting up monitoring systems for key indicators related to each scenario or incorporating scenario planning into regular strategic review sessions.

Debrief and Reflection:

1. Reflect on the Process: After completing the scenario planning exercise, facilitate a debrief session where leaders can reflect on the process. Discuss the insights gained, the challenges of thinking in scenarios, and how this exercise has affected their approach to strategic planning.

2. Discuss Flexibility and Preparedness: Lead a discussion on the importance of flexibility and preparedness in leadership. Explore how scenario planning helps build these qualities by forcing leaders to consider multiple possibilities and prepare for various outcomes.

3. Emphasize Continuous Learning: Highlight how scenario planning underscores the need for continuous learning and adaptability. Discuss strategies for staying informed about trends and developments that could impact future scenarios and how leaders can foster a culture of learning within their organizations to better navigate change.

4. Action Planning: Encourage leaders to think about how they can apply scenario planning in their leadership practice and within their teams. Discuss how they might use this tool to enhance decision-making, strategic planning, and team engagement.

Scenario Planning equips leaders with a powerful tool for navigating uncertainty and also reinforces the critical leadership qualities of foresight, flexibility, and a commitment to continuous improvement. By anticipating future changes and preparing strategic responses, leaders can better guide their organizations through the complexities of change and uncertainty, ensuring resilience and sustained success.

Chapter 8: Executive Presence and Branding

We now dive into the nuanced realms of executive presence and personal branding, two pivotal elements that profoundly influence leadership effectiveness and career progression in the modern business landscape. As leaders navigate the complexities of today's fast-paced, highly visible corporate environment, the ability to project confidence, authenticity, and a clear sense of purpose becomes increasingly vital. This chapter explores the essence of executive presence and personal branding, shedding light on their significance and the synergies between them in shaping a leader's impact and legacy.

Executive presence is often described as the intangible blend of gravitas, communication skills, and appearance that enables leaders to command attention, inspire confidence, and motivate action. It is the quality that makes stakeholders—be it employees, peers, or potential clients—sit up and take notice, engendering trust and respect. At its core, executive presence is about conveying leadership capability and credibility through every interaction, whether in boardroom discussions, team meetings, or public speaking engagements.

Personal branding, on the other hand, involves the deliberate effort to manage and communicate one's unique value proposition and professional identity to the outside world. It's about articulating what you stand for, your professional strengths, and how you differentiate yourself from others. A well-defined personal brand not only helps in establishing a leader's reputation within and outside the organization but also plays a critical role in career advancement by opening doors to new opportunities and networks.

The convergence of executive presence and personal branding forms a powerful duo that can significantly elevate a leader's effectiveness. Together, they create a compelling narrative about a leader's capabilities, vision, and values, making it easier to galvanize teams, drive change, and achieve strategic objectives. This chapter aims to provide readers with actionable insights into developing a strong executive presence and a distinctive personal brand. It covers strategies for honing communication skills, cultivating a professional image, and leveraging social media and other platforms to build and communicate one's brand.

Understanding and mastering the art of executive presence and personal branding is not merely about personal gain; it's about amplifying your ability to make a difference, influence outcomes, and contribute to the success of your organization. As we explore these concepts, we invite readers to reflect on their leadership journey, recognize their unique strengths, and consider how refining their presence and brand can unlock new levels of professional achievement and fulfillment.

Executive presence is an elusive yet critical attribute that distinguishes effective leaders, encapsulating the essence of how they are perceived and the influence they wield in various settings. At its heart, executive presence is the composite of confidence, authenticity, effective communication, emotional intelligence, professional appearance, inspirational leadership, and gravitas. These elements combine to create a leader who not only commands attention but also inspires confidence, credibility, and respect among peers, team members, and stakeholders.

Confidence stands at the forefront of executive presence, radiating a leader's self-assurance in their decisions and actions, which in turn instills a sense of trust and stability. This confidence, balanced with humility, prevents it from tipping into arrogance, maintaining a leader's relatability. Authenticity reinforces this trust, as leaders who are genuine and principled in their actions foster deeper loyalty and respect from their followers.

The ability to communicate effectively is another pillar of executive presence, encompassing clear, persuasive expression of ideas and active, empathetic listening. This skill ensures that a leader's message not only reaches their audience but also connects with them on a meaningful level. Emotional intelligence complements this by enabling leaders to navigate the complex web of interpersonal dynamics with grace, building robust relationships and a positive organizational culture.

A leader's professional appearance, though seemingly superficial, plays a significant role in shaping perceptions of their executive presence. An appearance that reflects the expectations of their role and aligns with organizational culture can significantly enhance a leader's credibility. Furthermore, the ability to inspire and engage others is central to executive presence, as it involves energizing teams with a compelling vision and fostering a commitment that drives performance.

Gravitas, or the projection of depth and dignity, adds a subtle strength to executive presence. It encompasses showing composure under pressure, decisiveness, and conveying a sense of authority that commands respect.

Developing executive presence is not an endpoint but a journey of continuous self-improvement. It requires a deliberate effort to cultivate these elements, striving for a balance that maximizes influence without sacrificing authenticity or empathy. Leaders who focus on enhancing their executive presence can significantly amplify their impact within their organizations and in the broader business landscape, navigating challenges with assurance and inspiring those around them to achieve collective success.

Cultivating executive presence is a deliberate and ongoing process that requires a focus on self-awareness and a commitment to continuous improvement. The journey to enhancing executive presence involves developing a deep understanding of oneself, honing interpersonal skills, and consistently projecting confidence and credibility. Here are strategies and tips to guide this developmental journey:

Start by engaging in self-reflection to gain a clearer understanding of your current strengths and areas for improvement. This can involve seeking feedback from colleagues, mentors, and coaches, as well as self-assessment tools. Understanding how others perceive you and recognizing your own self-perception gaps are critical steps in developing your executive presence.

Work on building your confidence through experiences and achievements. Confidence is often a result of competence. By seeking out challenging projects and opportunities for professional growth, you can build your skills and, consequently, your confidence. Remember, confidence also comes from accepting and learning from failures, not just celebrating successes.

Enhance your communication skills, focusing not only on the clarity and persuasiveness of your message but also on your listening skills. Effective communication is a two-way street that involves expressing your ideas clearly and being genuinely interested in others' perspectives. Practice active listening and empathy to build stronger connections and enhance your influence.

Develop your emotional intelligence by becoming more attuned to your own emotions and those of others. This involves practicing self-regulation, demonstrating empathy, and building social skills. Emotional intelligence is key to navigating complex interpersonal dynamics and leading with sensitivity and awareness.

Pay attention to your appearance and demeanor, ensuring they align with the professional image you wish to project. Your appearance should be appropriate for your role and industry, and your demeanor should reflect confidence and approachability. Remember, non-verbal cues such as posture, eye contact, and gestures also contribute significantly to how your presence is perceived.

Seek out opportunities to inspire and lead, whether through formal leadership roles or informal influence. Leadership is not just about holding a position of power; it's about motivating and guiding others towards a shared goal. Demonstrating your ability to lead with vision and integrity is a key component of executive presence.

Embrace continuous learning and development. The business landscape is constantly evolving, and staying informed and adaptable is crucial. Pursue professional development opportunities, stay abreast of industry trends, and be open to feedback and new ideas.

Cultivate resilience and composure, especially in challenging situations. Executive presence involves projecting stability and confidence, even under pressure. Developing coping strategies for stress and learning to maintain your composure in difficult situations can enhance your perceived leadership strength.

Remember that cultivating executive presence is a personal journey that takes time and effort. It's about aligning your inner values and strengths with your outward expressions and interactions. By focusing on self-awareness, continuous improvement, and the strategies outlined above, you can develop and enhance your executive presence, positioning yourself as a more effective and influential leader.

The essence of personal branding in the context of executive leadership is about crafting and conveying a coherent narrative that encapsulates an individual's values, strengths, and professional ethos. It is a strategic effort to position oneself in the minds of colleagues, stakeholders, and the broader professional community. Personal branding for executive leaders is not merely about self-promotion; it's a nuanced process of aligning one's personal values with their professional identity, ensuring that the two resonate in harmony and reinforce each other. This alignment is crucial for authenticity, which is the bedrock of a powerful personal brand.

Personal branding is increasingly relevant in today's digital and interconnected world, where the lines between personal and professional lives are often blurred. For executive leaders, a well-defined personal brand can serve as a differentiator in a competitive landscape, helping to establish credibility, influence, and thought leadership. It communicates not just what they do, but who they are and what they stand for, making it a critical component of their leadership toolkit.

At its core, personal branding involves a deep reflection on one's values, passions, and the unique contributions one can make to their field. It requires leaders to ask themselves what principles guide their decisions, how they want to impact their organization and industry, and what legacy they aspire to leave. The answers to these questions form the foundation of a personal brand, guiding how leaders present themselves in various forums, from speaking engagements and social media to networking events and beyond.

Personal branding is about consistency and coherence across all platforms and interactions. It's how leaders communicate their brand through their actions, words, and choices that build trust and respect among their audience. This consistency reinforces the leader's brand message, making it more memorable and impactful.

For executive leaders, personal branding also entails a responsibility to their organization. Their personal brand should complement and enhance the corporate brand, creating a synergy that benefits both the individual and the organization. This alignment can amplify the leader's effectiveness in driving organizational goals, attracting talent, and fostering a positive corporate culture.

In cultivating a personal brand, leaders must also be mindful of the evolving nature of their careers and the dynamic business environment. As such, personal branding is not a one-time effort but an ongoing process of adaptation and growth. Leaders should continuously seek feedback, stay abreast of industry trends, and refine their brand to reflect their evolving leadership journey.

The essence of personal branding for executive leaders lies in the deliberate alignment of personal values with professional identity.

It's a strategic endeavor that enhances leadership effectiveness, fosters authenticity, and positions leaders to navigate the complexities of the modern business landscape with confidence and clarity. By embracing personal branding, leaders can not only advance their careers but also make a meaningful impact on their organizations and the broader industry.

Developing your personal brand is a strategic process that involves deep self-reflection, clarity of purpose, and consistent expression of your identity across all professional interactions. It's about distinguishing yourself by identifying and articulating your strengths, unique value proposition (UVP), and leadership philosophy. Here's a guide to help you develop your personal brand:

1. Engage in Self-Reflection: Start with a thorough self-assessment to gain insights into your core values, passions, and what drives you. Reflect on questions such as what you are most passionate about in your work, the values that guide your decisions, and the impact you want to have through your leadership. Understanding these foundational elements is crucial for building a brand that is authentic and resonant.

2. Identify Your Strengths: Pinpoint your key strengths and the unique skills you bring to the table. Consider feedback from peers, performance reviews, and personal achievements to identify these strengths. Understanding what you excel at can help you focus your personal brand on areas where you naturally stand out.

3. Articulate Your Unique Value Proposition: Your UVP is what differentiates you from others in your field. It's a clear statement that describes the unique benefits you offer, who you serve, and why you're the best choice. Crafting a compelling UVP involves linking your strengths to the needs and challenges of your target audience, showcasing how you can address these in ways others cannot.

4. Define Your Leadership Philosophy: Your leadership philosophy is a reflection of how you view leadership and the principles that guide your approach. It encompasses your beliefs about motivating and inspiring others, making decisions, and achieving goals. Clearly articulating your leadership philosophy helps others understand what to expect from you and how you will guide your team or organization towards success.

5. Communicate Consistently: Once you have identified your strengths, UVP, and leadership philosophy, the next step is to communicate these aspects consistently across all platforms. This includes your professional bio, LinkedIn profile, speaking engagements, and day-to-day interactions. Consistency reinforces your personal brand, making it more recognizable and memorable to your audience.

6. Seek Feedback and Adapt: Personal branding is an ongoing process. Regularly seek feedback from trusted colleagues and mentors to understand how your brand is perceived and where there may be gaps between your intended and actual brand image. Be open to refining your brand as you grow and as the needs of your audience evolve.

7. Live Your Brand: Ultimately, the most powerful personal brand is one that is lived. Align your actions, decisions, and interactions with the key aspects of your personal brand. Authenticity in living your brand fosters trust and strengthens your leadership presence.

Developing your personal brand is not about crafting an image that you think others want to see. Instead, it's about uncovering and expressing your genuine self in a way that resonates with others and aligns with your professional goals. By following these steps, you can create a personal brand that not only distinguishes you as a leader but also amplifies your impact and influence in your field.

Effectively communicating and showcasing your personal brand requires a strategic approach that spans both online and offline platforms. It's about consistently conveying your values, strengths, and unique value proposition in a way that resonates with your target audience, whether they are colleagues, industry peers, or potential employers. Here's how to approach the communication of your personal brand:

Start with a clear and concise message that encapsulates the essence of your personal brand. This message should highlight your unique strengths, professional achievements, and the value you bring. Crafting a narrative that weaves together your professional journey, aspirations, and the impact you've made helps create a compelling story that people can connect with.

Online platforms offer a broad reach for personal brand communication. Ensure your LinkedIn profile, professional blog, or website accurately reflects your personal brand. This includes a professional photo, a bio that communicates your unique value proposition, and content that aligns with your expertise and leadership philosophy. Regularly update these platforms with your latest achievements, thought leadership articles, or insights that reinforce your brand.

Social media channels are powerful tools for brand communication, allowing you to engage with your audience in real-time. Share content that aligns with your brand, such as industry news, your viewpoints on trends, and insights from your professional experiences. Engaging with others' content thoughtfully can also amplify your presence and showcase your brand to a broader audience.

Networking, both online and offline, is vital in communicating your brand. Attend industry conferences, workshops, and other events where you can connect with like-minded professionals. Be prepared with an elevator pitch that succinctly communicates who you are, what you do, and what makes you unique. Cultivating a network of contacts who understand and value your brand can lead to new opportunities and collaborations.

Mentorship and public speaking are impactful ways to showcase your brand. Offering your expertise as a mentor or speaker not only positions you as an authority in your field but also demonstrates your commitment to giving back and influencing others positively. These interactions allow you to embody your brand and connect with others on a meaningful level.

Listening and adapting based on feedback is crucial in effectively communicating your brand. Pay attention to how others perceive and respond to your brand messaging. Be open to evolving your communication strategy to ensure it remains authentic and resonates with your audience.

Remember, consistency is key in brand communication. Every interaction, online post, and public appearance should reinforce the core elements of your personal brand. By integrating these techniques into your professional life, you can effectively communicate and showcase your personal brand, making a lasting impression on those you interact with and advancing your career.

Networking and relationship building are indispensable components of effective leadership, particularly for executive leaders who navigate complex environments and make decisions that shape the future of their organizations. The essence of networking in leadership transcends mere acquaintance-making; it involves cultivating meaningful, strategic relationships that can support personal and organizational growth. Here's an overview of the importance of networking and relationship building for executive leaders, along with the benefits of a robust professional network.

At its core, networking for leaders is about establishing and nurturing connections with individuals both within and outside their organizations. These connections can provide diverse perspectives, insights, and expertise, enriching a leader's understanding and approach to various challenges. Moreover, a strong network serves as a valuable resource for innovation, offering access to new ideas, practices, and technologies that can drive competitive advantage.

One of the key benefits of effective networking is the enhancement of a leader's ability to influence. Leaders often need to rally support for their visions and initiatives, and a broad, engaged network can amplify their influence, making it easier to garner buy-in and mobilize resources. Additionally, networking can facilitate collaboration and partnership opportunities, opening doors to strategic alliances that can propel organizational objectives forward.

Networking also plays a crucial role in talent attraction and retention. Executive leaders with extensive networks have better access to top talent, enabling them to identify and recruit individuals who can contribute to their organization's success. Furthermore, by connecting their teams with broader networks, leaders can provide valuable development opportunities, contributing to job satisfaction and employee retention.

Beyond immediate organizational benefits, networking supports leaders' personal and professional development. Interacting with a wide range of individuals exposes leaders to different leadership styles, problem-solving approaches, and management philosophies, fostering a continuous learning environment. These interactions can also offer insights into industry trends and potential disruptions, allowing leaders to better prepare and position their organizations for the future.

Effective networking requires a strategic and genuine approach. Leaders should seek to build relationships based on mutual respect and shared value rather than viewing networking as a transactional activity. This involves being proactive in reaching out, offering assistance, and maintaining contact over time, even when immediate benefits are not apparent.

Networking and relationship building are critical for executive leaders, offering a wealth of benefits that extend across personal development, influence, innovation, and organizational growth. By prioritizing and strategically engaging in networking, leaders can build a supportive ecosystem that enhances their effectiveness and contributes to the long-term success of their organizations.

Effective networking is an art that combines strategic outreach, genuine engagement, and thoughtful relationship management. For leaders and professionals seeking to expand their influence and opportunities, mastering effective networking strategies is essential. Here's practical advice on how to network effectively, focusing on making meaningful connections, maintaining relationships, and leveraging networks for career advancement.

Initiating meaningful connections starts with clarity about your networking goals. Whether seeking mentorship, industry insights, or potential collaborations, understanding what you hope to achieve helps tailor your networking efforts. Attend industry conferences, seminars, and other events where you can meet like-minded professionals. When introducing yourself, be concise yet informative about who you are and your professional interests, aiming to spark a conversation that goes beyond surface-level pleasantries.

Effective networking also hinges on the quality of interactions rather than the quantity. Focus on building fewer, more meaningful relationships rather than amassing a large number of superficial contacts. Show genuine interest in the people you meet by asking thoughtful questions and listening actively to their responses. This approach fosters deeper connections and is more likely to lead to mutually beneficial relationships.

Follow-up is critical in transforming initial meetings into lasting connections. After meeting someone new, reach out with a personalized message referencing your conversation. This not only shows that you value the interaction but also opens the door for future communication. Keep in touch by sharing articles, reports, or other resources relevant to their interests or field, and don't hesitate to reach out when you come across opportunities that might interest them.

Social media platforms, particularly LinkedIn, are powerful tools for networking. They allow you to connect with professionals worldwide, join industry-specific groups, and participate in discussions. Maintain an active presence by regularly updating your profile, publishing articles, or commenting on posts related to your field. This visibility can attract connections and opportunities to you.

Maintaining relationships over time requires effort and consistency. Schedule regular check-ins with your contacts, even if it's just a brief message or a quick coffee catch-up. Celebrate their achievements, offer support during challenges, and be willing to lend your expertise when needed. Reciprocity is key in networking; always look for ways to give back to your network.

Leveraging your network for career advancement involves being open about your professional goals and aspirations. However, ensure that your requests for assistance are specific and considerate of the other person's time and resources. Whether seeking advice, introductions, or feedback on ideas, approach your network with respect and gratitude for their support.

Remember that effective networking is a long-term investment in your professional journey. It's about building a community of colleagues and friends who support and inspire each other to grow. By focusing on meaningful connections, consistent engagement, and reciprocal value, you can cultivate a network that not only advances your career but also enriches your professional life.

In today's interconnected world, social media and digital platforms play a pivotal role in networking and personal branding. These tools offer unprecedented opportunities to connect with peers, industry leaders, and potential collaborators across the globe. By strategically leveraging digital networking, professionals can significantly enhance their visibility, establish their expertise, and build meaningful relationships. Here's a discussion on how to use social media and digital platforms effectively for networking and personal branding.

Social media platforms like LinkedIn, Twitter, and industry-specific forums are invaluable for professionals looking to expand their network. LinkedIn, in particular, stands out as a professional networking powerhouse, enabling users to showcase their career achievements, share insights, and connect with others in their field. To maximize LinkedIn's potential, ensure your profile is complete and reflects your professional brand. Regularly update your accomplishments, participate in discussions, and publish articles or posts that highlight your expertise and viewpoints.

Twitter can also be a powerful tool for networking and brand building, especially for staying on top of industry trends and engaging in real-time conversations with thought leaders and organizations. Follow relevant hashtags, contribute to discussions, and share content that aligns with your professional interests and brand. This active engagement can increase your visibility and position you as a knowledgeable participant in your field.

Beyond LinkedIn and Twitter, consider other digital platforms that align with your professional interests. For example, industry-specific forums, online communities, and blogs can offer more niche networking opportunities. Participating in these spaces can help you connect with like-minded professionals and deepen your knowledge in specific areas.

When using social media for networking, personalize your outreach. Whether you're connecting with someone new or engaging with content, personalized messages or comments can make a significant difference. Mention specific details that caught your attention or relate to your own experiences. This personalized approach fosters genuine connections and makes interactions more meaningful.

Content creation is another strategic aspect of digital networking. Sharing original content or curating relevant industry news can establish you as a thought leader in your field. It demonstrates your knowledge, insights, and commitment to your profession. Engage with your audience by responding to comments and participating in discussions, which further solidifies your professional relationships.

Privacy and professionalism are crucial when networking and building your brand online. Be mindful of the information you share and maintain a professional demeanor in all interactions. The digital footprint you leave can significantly impact your professional image and opportunities.

Digital networking should complement, not replace, traditional networking methods. While social media provides a convenient and wide-reaching platform for connecting with others, face-to-face interactions still hold immense value. Blend digital and traditional networking methods to maximize your reach and impact.

Social media and digital platforms are indispensable tools for modern networking and personal branding. By using these tools strategically, professionals can expand their networks, showcase their expertise, and engage with the global professional community. The key to success lies in being active, authentic, and strategic in your digital networking efforts.

Integrating executive presence and personal branding into daily leadership practice is a nuanced process that enhances a leader's influence, credibility, and effectiveness. It involves a deliberate effort to embody the qualities and values leaders wish to project in every facet of their leadership. Here's how leaders can weave executive presence and personal branding into their leadership practice and decision-making seamlessly.

Firstly, leaders should consistently demonstrate their core values in their actions, decisions, and interactions. This alignment between values and actions not only reinforces personal branding but also strengthens executive presence. Whether it's through transparency, innovation, empathy, or another value, showing these principles in action can solidify a leader's reputation and influence.

Effective communication is another cornerstone of integrating presence and branding. Developing a communication style that is authentic, clear, and resonates with the audience reinforces a leader's personal brand. This could involve storytelling, analogies, or directness, depending on the leader's unique style and the context of the communication.

Visual presentation, while not the essence of executive presence, plays a significant role in reinforcing a leader's personal brand. Dressing in a manner that reflects both the professional image suitable for the role and industry, and the leader's personal style, helps to cement their professional identity.

Strategic relationship building is crucial for expanding a leader's influence and extending their personal brand. By fostering relationships with individuals who share similar values and professional aspirations, and by offering support and mentorship, leaders can enrich their professional network and enhance their presence within their industry.

Decision-making processes offer an opportunity to align choices with personal branding and leadership philosophy. Leaders are encouraged to reflect on how their decisions reflect their personal brand and the message they wish to convey as a leader, ensuring coherence and integrity in their leadership approach.

The thoughtful use of social media platforms can serve to amplify a leader's personal brand and executive presence, allowing them to reach a broader audience. However, it's important to share content that aligns with the leader's professional image and values, maintaining consistency across digital and offline interactions.

A commitment to continuous learning and self-improvement is essential for sustaining executive presence and evolving a personal brand. Staying informed about industry trends, seeking feedback, and pursuing professional development opportunities demonstrate a leader's humility and adaptability.

Regular reflection on one's leadership practice, executive presence, and personal branding efforts is crucial for identifying successes and areas for improvement. Adjusting strategies as needed ensures that leadership practice and personal branding remain dynamic and effective in meeting the challenges of a changing environment.

By intentionally embodying the qualities associated with their personal brand and making strategic, value-aligned choices, leaders can enhance their effectiveness, influence, and impact on their organization and industry, ensuring that their leadership practice is not only effective but also authentic and resonant with their professional identity.

Evaluating and adjusting your strategy for executive presence and personal branding is a vital component of ongoing professional development, demanding a methodical approach to ensure alignment with evolving career goals and the dynamic professional environment. This process starts with the gathering of continuous feedback from a broad spectrum of sources such as peers, mentors, direct reports, and clients. Incorporating tools like 360-degree feedback surveys offers a holistic view of how others perceive your executive presence and personal brand, highlighting both strengths and areas for improvement.

Complementing external insights, self-assessment and reflection are crucial. Assess your authenticity and confidence across professional interactions and whether these engagements reflect your intended brand. Reflecting on your leadership philosophy and values, and their manifestation in your actions, provides personal insight into the effectiveness of your branding efforts.

An objective evaluation against your career goals and objectives is also essential. Analyze whether your current branding strategy is facilitating progress towards these aims or identify any discrepancies that may need addressing. This could involve refining your unique value proposition to better meet your audience's needs.

The opportunities that emerge as a result of your branding efforts serve as significant indicators of their effectiveness. An uptick in relevant professional opportunities, such as job offers, networking invitations, or speaking engagements, suggests that your executive presence and personal brand are resonating with your target audience.

In today's digital age, a review of your online presence is indispensable. Ensure your digital footprint, including social media profiles and professional publications, accurately represents your professional identity and enhances your executive presence.

Based on feedback and self-reflection, pinpoint areas needing adjustment. This may involve improving specific skills, tweaking your communication approach, or redefining your value proposition to align more closely with your career aspirations. Be prepared to evolve your personal brand as you progress in your career and as market dynamics change.

After implementing adjustments, establish new benchmarks to measure progress. Setting specific, measurable goals related to aspects like networking, visibility, or leadership impact can help in tracking the effectiveness of these adjustments over time.

Consider professional development opportunities to bolster areas of your executive presence and personal branding needing enhancement. Engaging in workshops, courses, or coaching can provide the skills and insights needed to refine your strategy further.

This iterative process of evaluation and adjustment is fundamental to maintaining a relevant and impactful executive presence and personal brand. By actively seeking feedback, reflecting on your professional practice, and being willing to adapt, you can ensure that your personal branding remains a potent asset in achieving your professional goals and leaving a lasting impact in your field.

It's clear that these elements are indispensable in defining a leader's impact and opening doors to new career opportunities. Executive presence, with its emphasis on confidence, authenticity, and the ability to inspire and engage, allows leaders to command respect and influence outcomes effectively. Meanwhile, personal branding serves as a strategic tool for leaders to communicate their unique value and vision, setting them apart in a competitive landscape.

Throughout this journey, we've underscored the transformative power of integrating executive presence and personal branding into daily leadership practice. By engaging with the exercises provided, readers have the opportunity to actively cultivate their executive presence, refine their personal branding, and extend their professional reach. These practical steps are designed not only to enhance immediate leadership effectiveness but also to lay the groundwork for sustained career growth and development.

Building and maintaining a strong executive identity is an ongoing process that demands intentionality and commitment. At the heart of this endeavor is the importance of authenticity—being true to one's values and convictions. Authenticity ensures that your executive presence and personal brand resonate genuinely with others, fostering trust and loyalty among peers, subordinates, and stakeholders.

Continuous learning and adaptation are also crucial in this dynamic process. The business landscape and professional roles are ever evolving, necessitating that leaders remain agile, open to new ideas, and proactive in acquiring new skills. This commitment to growth not only enriches personal development but also ensures that leaders can effectively navigate the complexities of their roles and industries.

Strategic networking, too, plays a vital role in amplifying executive presence and personal branding. By building and nurturing a diverse professional network, leaders can access new insights, opportunities, and support systems that propel them forward. Effective networking, grounded in genuine interactions and mutual value exchange, extends the reach of your personal brand and solidifies your position as a thought leader in your field.

Executive presence and personal branding are critical components of impactful leadership and career advancement. By actively developing these aspects through the exercises provided and embracing authenticity, continuous learning, and strategic networking, leaders can forge a powerful executive identity. This identity not only elevates their immediate leadership impact but also positions them for long-term success and fulfillment in their professional journey.

Exercises for Chapter 8: Executive Presence and Branding

Exercise 20: Enhancing Your Executive Presence

Objective: This exercise is designed to help you actively enhance your executive presence by focusing on self-awareness, communication, and visibility.

Step 1: Self-Reflection

- Allocate 15 minutes to reflect on aspects of your current executive presence. Consider your confidence level, communication style, and how you believe others perceive you in professional settings.

- Write down three strengths of your executive presence and three areas for improvement.

Step 2: Communication Practice

- Select a recent professional interaction where you felt your communication could have been more effective. Revisit this scenario and write down what you said or did.

- Now, rewrite the script for this interaction, incorporating your strengths and addressing the areas for improvement identified in Step 1. Focus on clarity, confidence, and empathy.

Step 3: Visibility Action Plan

- Identify one opportunity in the next week to increase your visibility within your organization or industry. This could be leading a meeting, contributing to a company newsletter, or participating in a professional networking event.

- Plan your involvement in this opportunity, outlining how you will use it to showcase your improved executive presence. Consider how you will communicate, what value you can bring to the interaction, and how you can leave a positive, lasting impression.

Step 4: Reflection and Adjustment

- After completing the visibility action plan, reflect on the experience. What went well? What challenges did you face? How did others respond to you?

- Based on this reflection, adjust your approach for future interactions. Identify one thing you will continue to do and one thing you will change to further enhance your executive presence.

By actively engaging in this exercise, you will take tangible steps towards enhancing your executive presence, leveraging self-reflection, strategic communication, and increased visibility to make a more impactful impression on those around you. Remember, executive presence is an ongoing journey of personal and professional development.

Exercise 21: Personal Branding Statement Exercise

Objective: This exercise aims to guide leaders in crafting a concise and impactful personal branding statement that effectively encapsulates their professional identity and value. The personal branding statement is a vital tool in communicating your unique contributions and aspirations to peers, superiors, and the broader professional community.

Step 1: Reflect on Your Core Values and Strengths

Begin with a period of reflection on your core values and strengths. What principles guide your professional actions and decisions? Which personal strengths do you most frequently rely on in your leadership role? Write these down as they will form the foundation of your branding statement.

Step 2: Identify Your Unique Value Proposition (UVP)

Consider what sets you apart from others in your field. Reflect on the unique combination of skills, experiences, and perspectives you bring to your role. How do these elements translate into tangible benefits for your organization or industry? Summarize your thoughts to clarify your UVP.

Step 3: Articulate Your Professional Aspirations

Think about your professional goals and aspirations. What impact do you hope to achieve through your leadership? How do you want to influence your field or organization? Understanding your aspirations will help shape a forward-looking component of your branding statement.

Step 4: Draft Your Personal Branding Statement

Using the insights gathered from the previous steps, begin drafting your personal branding statement. Aim for a statement that is no more than a few sentences long, encapsulating your core values, strengths, UVP, and professional aspirations. Keep it clear, compelling, and authentic to who you are as a leader.

Example: "As a dedicated [Your Profession/Role] with a passion for [Core Value] and [Another Core Value], I leverage my [Specific Strength] and [Another Strength] to drive [Specific Benefit] for [Your Organization/Industry]. Committed to [Professional Aspiration], I aim to [Impact You Wish to Make], fostering [Outcome] in every endeavor."

Step 5: Refine and Finalize

Review your draft and refine it for clarity, impact, and authenticity. Ensure that it accurately reflects your professional identity and speaks to your target audience. You may wish to seek feedback from trusted colleagues or mentors to further hone your statement.

Step 6: Put Your Branding Statement into Action

Consider ways to integrate your personal branding statement into your professional activities. This could include updating your LinkedIn profile, incorporating it into your professional bio, or using it as an anchor in networking conversations. Consistently using your branding statement will reinforce your professional identity and value to others.

By completing this exercise, leaders will have developed a personal branding statement that not only highlights their unique contributions and goals but also serves as a powerful tool in building their professional presence and opening doors to new opportunities. Remember, your personal branding statement should evolve as you grow in your career, so revisit and adjust it as necessary to reflect your current aspirations and achievements.

Exercise 22: Networking Strategy Plan

This exercise is aimed at helping leaders develop a comprehensive networking strategy that outlines their goals, identifies target connections, and creates an action plan for building and nurturing a robust professional network.

- Step 1: Define Your Networking Goals: Begin by clarifying what you aim to achieve through your networking efforts. Goals can range from seeking mentorship, gaining industry insights, finding collaboration opportunities, to enhancing your personal brand. Being specific about your goals will guide your networking strategy and make your efforts more focused and effective.

- Step 2: Identify Target Connections: Based on your networking goals, identify the types of professionals you need to connect with. This could include industry leaders, peers in similar roles, potential mentors, or professionals with specific expertise. Make a list of these target connection types and consider why each is important to your networking goals.

- Step 3: Research Potential Contacts: Conduct research to identify specific individuals who fit your target connection criteria. Utilize LinkedIn, professional associations, and industry events to find potential contacts. Create a list of names along with any relevant information, such as their professional background, common connections, or interests.

- Step 4: Develop Your Engagement Strategy: For each target connection, develop a personalized engagement strategy. This could involve connecting on LinkedIn with a personalized message, engaging with their published content, or seeking introductions through mutual connections. Plan how you will introduce yourself and what value you can offer to initiate a meaningful interaction.

- Step 5: Create an Action Plan: Outline a timeline and action steps for reaching out to your target connections. Set realistic goals for how many new connections you will attempt to make each week or month. Include follow-up actions to deepen connections, such as inviting them for a virtual coffee chat, attending the same industry webinar, or sharing relevant articles and resources.

- Step 6: Measure and Adjust Your Strategy: Keep track of your networking activities and the outcomes of each interaction. Evaluate the effectiveness of your strategy in meeting your networking goals. Are you making the desired connections? Are these connections bringing you closer to your goals? Based on this assessment, adjust your strategy and actions as needed to improve your results.

- Step 7: Foster and Maintain Relationships: Networking is not a one-time activity but an ongoing process of relationship-building. Plan regular check-ins with your new connections to share updates, offer support, or collaborate on mutual interests. Keep notes on key details from your interactions to personalize future communications.

By completing this exercise, leaders will have a structured networking strategy that not only helps in expanding their professional network but also ensures that these connections are meaningful and aligned with their career objectives. Remember, the quality of connections often outweighs quantity, so focus on building relationships that are mutually beneficial and supportive of your professional growth.

Chapter 9: Global Executive Leadership Coaching

In the tapestry of today's rapidly evolving business environment, the ability of executive leaders to adopt a global perspective is not just an asset; it's a necessity. The interconnectedness of economies, the digital revolution, and the mobility of talent across borders have underscored the importance of understanding and navigating the complexities of the global marketplace. This chapter introduces the concept of global executive leadership, highlighting the critical need for leaders to embrace cultural diversity, stay abreast of global trends, and develop strategies to amplify their influence on the world stage.

The objectives of this section are threefold. First, it aims to deepen leaders' understanding of cultural diversity and its impact on leadership practices. In a world where teams, clients, and stakeholders can span continents, an appreciation for and understanding of cultural nuances can bridge divides, foster collaboration, and drive innovation. Leaders equipped with cultural intelligence can navigate the subtleties of global business dynamics more effectively, building cohesive teams and partnerships across cultural boundaries.

Second, this chapter will explore the global trends that are reshaping the landscape of leadership. From technological advancements and shifting economic powers to environmental challenges and social movements, leaders must be attuned to the forces shaping our world. Recognizing these trends is crucial for anticipating changes, seizing opportunities, and mitigating risks on a global scale. This section will provide insights into how leaders can stay informed and adapt their strategies to thrive in an ever-changing global context.

We will dive into strategies for expanding a leader's influence globally. In a competitive and complex international arena, leaders must leverage their vision, expertise, and networks to make an impact. This involves not only mastering the art of cross-cultural communication but also embodying a global mindset in decision-making and strategy formulation. Leaders will learn how to project their influence beyond their immediate environment, contributing to their organization's global footprint and driving positive change in the wider world.

By engaging with the concepts and strategies outlined in this chapter, leaders will be better positioned to navigate the intricacies of global executive leadership. Embracing a global perspective is imperative for today's leaders, enabling them to lead with foresight, agility, and a deepened awareness of the diverse world in which we operate. This chapter serves as a guide for those ready to take on the challenges and opportunities of leading in the global arena, equipping them with the knowledge and tools to expand their influence and drive success on a global scale.

In global leadership, cultural diversity encompasses the varied tapestry of human backgrounds, including but not limited to nationality, ethnicity, language, religion, and social norms. It represents the multitude of perspectives, values, and practices that individuals bring to professional and social interactions. For leaders in a globalized business environment, grasping the essence of cultural diversity is foundational to fostering inclusive, dynamic, and effective organizations.

The significance of cultural diversity in global leadership cannot be overstated. It introduces a rich array of viewpoints and approaches to problem-solving, driving innovation and creativity within teams and organizations. Diverse teams are shown to be more adept at analyzing issues from multiple angles, leading to more robust decision-making processes. Furthermore, leaders who embrace and effectively manage cultural diversity can tap into a wider range of markets and customer bases, enhancing the global reach and relevance of their organizations.

The benefits of cultural diversity come with their own set of challenges. Differences in communication styles, decision-making processes, and conflict resolution methods can lead to misunderstandings and friction within teams. Leaders must navigate these challenges with sensitivity and adaptability, striving to create an environment where all team members feel valued and understood. This involves not only recognizing and respecting cultural differences but also actively seeking to understand the underlying values and motivations that drive those differences.

Cultural diversity offers leaders the opportunity to demonstrate and develop global competence—an essential skill in today's interconnected world. Leaders with global competence possess the awareness, knowledge, and skills to operate effectively across cultures. They are adept at building cross-cultural relationships, communicating effectively across language and cultural barriers, and adapting leadership styles to meet the needs of diverse teams.

To navigate cultural diversity effectively, leaders can employ several strategies. These include investing in cultural intelligence training for themselves and their teams, fostering open and inclusive communication practices, and creating policies and practices that support diversity and inclusion. Additionally, leaders can seek out diverse mentors and advisors who can provide insights and guidance on navigating cultural nuances.

Cultural diversity in leadership is a complex yet invaluable aspect of global business. Understanding and effectively managing cultural diversity can unlock tremendous potential for innovation, market expansion, and team performance. It requires leaders to embark on a continuous journey of learning and adaptation, guided by empathy, respect, and an unwavering commitment to fostering an inclusive workplace. Embracing cultural diversity is not merely a strategic advantage—it is a critical component of leadership excellence in the 21st century.

Developing Cultural Intelligence (CQ) is increasingly recognized as a critical skill for leaders in the global business landscape. Cultural Intelligence represents a leader's ability to function effectively across national, ethnic, and organizational cultures. It encompasses understanding cultural norms and expectations, adapting to new cultural settings, and interacting successfully with individuals from diverse backgrounds. CQ is composed of three primary components: cognitive, motivational, and behavioral, each playing a vital role in a leader's global competence.

Cognitive CQ refers to a leader's knowledge and understanding of different cultures, including their economic, legal, and social systems. This component emphasizes the importance of being well-informed about the cultures one interacts with, understanding how cultural norms influence business practices, communication styles, and decision-making processes. Leaders with high cognitive CQ can anticipate potential cultural misunderstandings and effectively navigate the complexities of multicultural interactions.

Developing cognitive CQ involves dedicated learning and exposure. Leaders can enhance this aspect of their CQ by engaging in cultural studies, participating in cross-cultural training programs, and seeking firsthand experiences in different cultural settings. Staying informed about global events and trends also contributes to a nuanced understanding of how cultures intersect and evolve.

Motivational CQ centers on a leader's interest, drive, and confidence to adapt to multicultural situations. It reflects an intrinsic motivation to learn and engage with different cultures, underpinned by a genuine curiosity and openness towards cultural diversity. Leaders with strong motivational CQ are propelled by a desire to understand and appreciate the perspectives and experiences of others, fostering a deep respect for cultural differences.

Enhancing motivational CQ requires introspection and a commitment to personal growth. Leaders can cultivate this component by reflecting on their attitudes towards cultural differences, seeking out diverse experiences that challenge their worldviews, and setting personal goals for cultural learning and engagement.

Behavioral CQ involves a leader's ability to adapt their behavior and communication styles in culturally diverse settings. This component is about the practical application of cultural knowledge and motivation, demonstrating respect and empathy through one's actions. Leaders with high behavioral CQ can effectively adjust their leadership style, negotiation tactics, and conflict resolution approaches to align with different cultural expectations, thereby building rapport and trust across cultures.

Improving behavioral CQ demands practice and feedback. Leaders can work on this aspect by experimenting with different communication styles and observing their impact, actively seeking feedback from cultural mentors or peers, and being mindful of non-verbal cues and social norms in diverse settings.

Developing Cultural Intelligence is an essential endeavor for global leaders aiming to navigate the complexities of today's interconnected world effectively. By focusing on the cognitive, motivational, and behavioral components of CQ, leaders can enhance their ability to understand, respect, and engage with cultural diversity. This not only enriches their personal leadership practice but also contributes to building inclusive, innovative, and successful global organizations. Continuous learning, openness to new experiences, and a genuine commitment to understanding others are the hallmarks of a culturally intelligent leader.

Navigating and leveraging cultural differences in international business contexts requires a nuanced understanding of the complexities inherent in cross-cultural interactions. Effective strategies encompass a range of practices from cultivating cultural intelligence to fostering inclusive communication. Here's how leaders can navigate these differences effectively.

Developing a deep understanding of the cultures you interact with is foundational. This involves more than just awareness of basic customs or etiquette; it requires an in-depth exploration of cultural values, communication styles, decision-making processes, and business practices. Immersing oneself in the culture through literature, media, and direct engagement can provide valuable insights that go beyond surface-level knowledge.

Cultivating empathy and openness is critical when engaging with diverse cultures. Approaching interactions with a genuine willingness to understand and appreciate different perspectives fosters trust and respect. Empathy enables leaders to see beyond their own cultural lenses, recognize the validity of other viewpoints, and find common ground.

Active listening plays a pivotal role in cross-cultural communication. By paying close attention and showing respect for the speaker's viewpoint, leaders can avoid misunderstandings and gain deeper insights into cultural nuances. This attentiveness also signals respect for the other culture, which is crucial in building rapport.

Adapting communication styles to fit the cultural context is another essential strategy. Some cultures prefer direct and explicit communication, while others rely on context and non-verbal cues to convey meaning. Being flexible and adjusting your communication style can prevent miscommunications and foster clearer, more effective exchanges.

Building a diverse team within your organization can provide a competitive advantage in international business. A team with members from various cultural backgrounds brings a wealth of perspectives that can enhance problem-solving, creativity, and innovation. Additionally, it creates an environment where cultural differences are not just accepted but valued.

Seeking feedback from peers or mentors familiar with the culture can offer leaders valuable insights into their cross-cultural interactions. This feedback can highlight areas of success and those requiring improvement, guiding leaders in refining their approach to navigating cultural differences.

Continuous learning and self-reflection are key to effectively leveraging cultural differences. The global business landscape is dynamic, with cultural norms and business practices continually evolving. Leaders must commit to ongoing education and reflection on their experiences to adapt their strategies and maintain effectiveness in international contexts.

Navigating and leveraging cultural differences in international business requires a multifaceted approach that emphasizes understanding, empathy, adaptability, and continuous growth. By employing these strategies, leaders can turn cultural diversity into a strategic asset, driving success and innovation in the global marketplace.

In today's rapidly evolving world, several key global trends are significantly impacting businesses and, by extension, executive leadership. Understanding these trends is crucial for leaders aiming to navigate the complexities of the global marketplace effectively and steer their organizations towards long-term success.

Technological advancements are at the forefront of global trends shaping the business landscape. The rise of artificial intelligence, machine learning, blockchain, and the Internet of Things (IoT) is transforming industries, from automating processes to enabling new business models. For executive leaders, this means not only investing in the right technologies but also fostering a culture of innovation and agility within their organizations to leverage these advancements competitively.

Economic shifts are another critical global trend, with the rise of emerging markets and the changing dynamics of international trade. The economic ascent of countries in Asia, Africa, and Latin America is creating new opportunities and challenges for businesses. Executive leaders must navigate these shifts by developing global strategies that capitalize on growth opportunities in these regions while also managing the risks associated with geopolitical and economic volatility.

Sustainability concerns are increasingly becoming a central consideration for businesses worldwide. Issues such as climate change, resource depletion, and social inequality are prompting a reevaluation of business practices. Consumers, employees, and investors are demanding more responsible and sustainable approaches to business. For leaders, this means integrating sustainability into the core of their business strategy, balancing economic success with environmental stewardship and social responsibility.

The trend towards greater digitalization and remote work, accelerated by the COVID-19 pandemic, has also had a profound impact on leadership. The shift to remote and hybrid work models has challenged traditional leadership and management practices, requiring leaders to find new ways to motivate, engage, and oversee their teams in a digital environment. This trend emphasizes the need for leaders to develop strong digital communication skills and to cultivate a culture of trust and accountability.

The increasing importance of diversity, equity, and inclusion (DEI) in the workplace is a trend that leaders cannot afford to ignore. As global awareness of social justice issues grows, businesses are expected to play a leading role in promoting diversity and ensuring equitable opportunities for all employees. This requires leaders to actively work towards creating an inclusive culture where diverse perspectives are valued and contribute to the organization's innovation and resilience.

These global trends—technological advancements, economic shifts, sustainability concerns, the move towards digitalization and remote work, and the emphasis on diversity, equity, and inclusion—are reshaping the landscape of executive leadership. Leaders who recognize and adapt to these trends can guide their organizations to navigate the challenges and opportunities of the global marketplace successfully, ensuring long-term sustainability and growth.

The global trends impacting businesses today—technological advancements, economic shifts, sustainability concerns, the rise of digital and remote work, and the growing emphasis on diversity, equity, and inclusion—are also reshaping leadership roles and responsibilities. These changes demand that leaders adopt adaptive strategies and innovative approaches to navigate the complexities of the modern business environment successfully.

Technological advancements necessitate leaders to not only be conversant with the latest technologies but also to possess the foresight to understand how these innovations can be harnessed to drive business growth and efficiency. This involves a shift from traditional leadership roles to becoming champions of innovation and change, encouraging a culture where experimentation and agility are valued. Leaders must foster environments that stimulate creativity, ensuring their teams are equipped with the skills needed to thrive in a tech-driven landscape.

The economic shifts, marked by the rise of emerging markets and changing trade dynamics, require leaders to develop a more global outlook. Adapting to these changes means cultivating a deep understanding of diverse markets and customizing strategies to meet varied consumer needs and regulatory environments. Leaders must navigate these economic shifts with a balanced approach, leveraging global opportunities while mitigating risks associated with geopolitical and economic uncertainties.

Sustainability concerns are pushing leaders to integrate environmental and social governance into their core business strategy. This transition requires leaders to think beyond short-term profit and consider the long-term impact of their business operations on the planet and society. Adopting sustainable practices necessitates innovative thinking to reconcile profitability with environmental stewardship and social responsibility, requiring leaders to champion sustainability initiatives and embed them into the organizational culture.

The trend towards digitalization and remote work has transformed traditional notions of the workplace, necessitating leaders to adapt their management styles. Effective leadership in a digital and remote context emphasizes clear communication, trust, and flexibility. Leaders must leverage digital tools to maintain team cohesion and ensure productivity, fostering a culture that supports work-life balance and employee well-being in a remote setting.

The emphasis on diversity, equity, and inclusion demands leaders to be more intentional in creating inclusive environments. This involves recognizing and addressing unconscious biases, promoting diverse hiring and advancement practices, and ensuring all voices are heard and valued. Leaders must champion DEI initiatives, understanding that diverse and inclusive teams are more innovative, resilient, and better positioned to succeed in a global marketplace.

Adapting leadership to global changes requires a multifaceted approach that embraces innovation, global awareness, sustainability, digital adeptness, and inclusivity. Leaders must be proactive in evolving their strategies and approaches, staying ahead of trends, and preparing their organizations to navigate the challenges and opportunities presented by the global business landscape. This adaptive and innovative leadership approach is essential for driving success and ensuring long-term sustainability in an ever-changing world.

Future-proofing leadership skills in a rapidly changing global landscape requires a proactive approach to developing competencies that align with the evolving demands of the business environment. Agility, resilience, and a global mindset stand out as critical attributes for leaders aiming to navigate these changes successfully. Here's how leaders can cultivate these essential skills:

- Cultivate Agility: Agility is the ability to rapidly adapt and respond to change. Leaders can develop agility by fostering a culture of continuous learning and experimentation within their teams. Encouraging innovation and being open to new ideas and approaches allows leaders and their organizations to pivot quickly in response to changing market dynamics. To enhance agility, leaders should also practice scenario planning, envisioning various future states and preparing strategies to address them, ensuring they can navigate uncertainty with confidence.

- Build Resilience: Resilience is crucial for withstanding the pressures and setbacks inherent in a volatile business environment. Leaders can build resilience by maintaining a positive outlook, even in the face of challenges, and viewing failures as opportunities for growth and learning. Developing a strong support network, both professionally and personally, can provide leaders with the resources and encouragement needed to persevere. Additionally, prioritizing well-being and stress management helps maintain the mental and emotional strength necessary to lead effectively through tough times.

- Foster a Global Mindset: A global mindset involves seeing beyond one's immediate context and considering the broader, international implications of business decisions. Leaders can develop a global mindset by actively seeking experiences and knowledge that broaden their understanding of different cultures, markets, and global trends. This can include international assignments, cross-cultural training, or collaborating with multinational teams. Understanding and appreciating diversity in all its forms enhances a leader's ability to operate effectively across boundaries and leverage the opportunities presented by globalization.

- Enhance Emotional Intelligence: Emotional intelligence (EQ) is the ability to understand and manage one's own emotions and to recognize and influence the emotions of others. High EQ is invaluable for leaders in managing cross-cultural teams, navigating complex stakeholder relationships, and leading with empathy. Leaders can enhance their EQ by practicing active listening, seeking feedback on their interpersonal skills, and engaging in self-reflection to better understand their emotional responses and triggers.

- Improve Technological Literacy: As technology continues to drive change across all aspects of business, leaders must stay informed about technological trends and understand their implications. Developing technological literacy allows leaders to identify opportunities for innovation and ensure their organizations remain competitive. Leaders don't need to be tech experts but should be knowledgeable enough to make informed decisions and lead tech-driven change initiatives.

- Strengthen Strategic Thinking: The ability to think strategically about the long-term direction and success of an organization is more important than ever. Leaders can strengthen their strategic thinking by regularly analyzing industry trends, competitive landscapes, and internal strengths and weaknesses. Engaging in strategic dialogues with peers, mentors, and experts outside the organization can also provide new perspectives and insights.

Future-proofing leadership skills requires a commitment to ongoing development and adaptability. By focusing on cultivating agility, resilience, a global mindset, emotional intelligence, technological literacy, and strategic thinking, leaders can equip themselves with the competencies needed to succeed in a rapidly changing global landscape. These skills not only enable leaders to navigate the challenges of today but also to seize the opportunities of tomorrow, ensuring sustained success and relevance in the global marketplace.

Expanding leadership influence on a global scale necessitates cultivating a global network of contacts, a strategic endeavor that opens doors to new insights, opportunities, and collaborations beyond local boundaries. Building and maintaining a global network involves intentional efforts to connect with professionals across different regions, industries, and cultures, fostering relationships that can provide mutual benefits over time.

The importance of such a network lies in its ability to enhance a leader's perspective, providing a broader understanding of global trends, cultural nuances, and market dynamics. A well-cultivated global network serves as a vital resource for knowledge exchange, offering access to diverse viewpoints and expertise that can inform decision-making and innovation. Moreover, these connections can become pivotal during international expansions, entering new markets, or when seeking partners for cross-border projects.

To build a global network, leaders should first leverage digital platforms like LinkedIn, which facilitate connections with professionals worldwide. Engaging with content, participating in discussions, and joining industry-specific groups can raise a leader's profile and attract connections with shared interests. Attending international conferences, seminars, and workshops also provides opportunities to meet peers from various countries, laying the groundwork for meaningful professional relationships.

Once connections are made, maintaining these relationships requires regular engagement. This can include sharing relevant articles, reports, or insights that might be of interest to your contacts or reaching out with personalized messages to check in or congratulate them on recent achievements. Such interactions, though seemingly small, keep the relationship alive and ensure you remain top of mind.

Another effective strategy is to offer value without expecting immediate returns. This could involve providing advice, making introductions, or offering support on projects. By being generous with your knowledge and resources, you create a positive impression that fosters goodwill and reciprocity, strengthening the bond between you and your global contacts.

Collaboration is also key to deepening global connections. Working on joint projects, co-authoring articles, or participating in panel discussions together can solidify relationships, allowing you to demonstrate your expertise and commitment to mutual success. These collaborative efforts not only benefit all parties involved but also expand your visibility and influence within the global community.

Cultural sensitivity and understanding play a crucial role in building and maintaining a global network. Being mindful of cultural differences, communication styles, and social norms is essential in fostering respectful and productive interactions. Taking the time to learn about the cultures of your contacts demonstrates respect and enhances mutual understanding.

Expanding leadership influence on a global scale through building a global network is a strategic process that requires leveraging digital tools, engaging in international events, maintaining regular contact, offering value, collaborating on projects, and practicing cultural sensitivity. By investing time and effort into cultivating these global relationships, leaders can unlock a wealth of opportunities and insights, driving success and innovation in an increasingly interconnected world.

Leading multicultural and geographically dispersed teams presents unique challenges and opportunities. Success in this environment hinges on a leader's ability to foster an atmosphere of open communication, inclusivity, and collaboration. Here's how leaders can excel in guiding diverse teams across different regions.

Effective communication is the cornerstone of leading dispersed teams. Leaders must establish clear channels of communication that accommodate different time zones and leverage technology to bridge geographical gaps. Regular video conferences, team chats, and digital collaboration tools can help maintain a sense of connection and ensure that all team members are aligned with the team's goals and progress. It's also important to be mindful of language barriers and cultural nuances in communication styles, opting for clarity and simplicity to avoid misunderstandings.

Creating an inclusive team culture is crucial when leading multicultural teams. This involves valuing and respecting each team member's unique background, perspectives, and contributions. Leaders should encourage team members to share their cultural insights and experiences, fostering a learning environment where diversity is seen as a strength. Implementing team-building activities that celebrate cultural diversity can also enhance mutual respect and understanding among team members.

Promoting collaboration in geographically dispersed teams requires intentional structuring of team interactions and projects. Leaders should create opportunities for team members to work together on tasks that leverage their diverse skills and perspectives. This might involve pairing team members from different cultures on projects or setting up cross-functional teams to tackle complex challenges. Encouraging peer-to-peer learning and support can also strengthen team cohesion and facilitate knowledge sharing.

Recognizing and accommodating cultural differences in work practices and expectations is another key aspect of leading multicultural teams. This includes understanding variations in communication preferences, decision-making processes, and attitudes towards hierarchy and authority. Leaders can address these differences by setting clear expectations, adapting leadership styles to suit the team's cultural dynamics, and being flexible in their approach to work arrangements and deadlines.

Fostering a sense of belonging and engagement among team members, regardless of their location, is essential. This can be achieved by ensuring that remote team members have equal access to information, resources, and opportunities for professional development. Regular feedback and recognition of each team member's contributions can also boost morale and engagement.

Leaders themselves must commit to continuous learning and development in cross-cultural competence. This includes seeking feedback on their leadership approach, engaging in cultural training, and staying informed about global trends that may impact their team. By modeling a commitment to growth and openness to different cultures, leaders can inspire their teams to embrace diversity and work together more effectively.

Leading multicultural and geographically dispersed teams successfully requires a strategic approach centered on effective communication, inclusivity, and collaboration. By embracing these best practices, leaders can harness the full potential of their diverse teams, driving innovation, and achieving superior results in the global business landscape.

Developing and implementing a global strategy that aligns with an organization's vision while leveraging international opportunities involves a comprehensive approach. This strategy must consider the complexities of operating across diverse markets and cultural landscapes, requiring a blend of strategic foresight, adaptability, and a deep understanding of global dynamics. Here's a structured approach to crafting a global strategy:

1. Articulate a Clear Global Vision: Start by defining a clear and compelling global vision that aligns with the organization's overall mission and values. This vision should reflect the organization's aspirations on the global stage, including the markets it aims to serve, the impact it seeks to have, and how it intends to differentiate itself from competitors. A well-articulated global vision provides a guiding north star for all international operations and decisions.

2. Conduct Thorough Global Market Analysis: Understanding the landscape in which you operate is crucial. Conduct an in-depth analysis of potential markets, including economic, political, social, and technological factors that could impact your business. This analysis should also cover market needs, customer behaviors, and competitive dynamics. Insights gained from this analysis will inform strategic decisions about where to compete and how to position your offerings.

3. Identify Your Unique Value Proposition (UVP): In the context of your global vision and market analysis, define your UVP for the international market. Your UVP should address why customers in different regions should choose your offerings over local competitors. It may involve innovation, cost advantages, customization to local needs, or superior customer

service. A compelling UVP is critical for differentiating your organization in a crowded global market.

4. Tailor Strategies to Local Markets: While a global strategy provides overall direction, success often depends on the ability to adapt and tailor approaches to each local market. This could involve customizing products or services to meet local needs, adapting marketing strategies to resonate with local cultures, or adjusting operational tactics to comply with local regulations. Flexibility and local relevance are key to winning in diverse markets.

5. Build a Robust Global Infrastructure: Effective global operations require a supportive infrastructure. This includes establishing local offices or partnerships, developing efficient logistics and supply chain networks, and implementing IT systems that support global coordination. A strong infrastructure enables the organization to execute its global strategy effectively and responsively.

6. Foster a Global Mindset Among Leadership and Teams: Cultivating a global mindset within your organization is essential for implementing a global strategy successfully. This involves training leaders and teams to understand and appreciate cultural differences, encouraging cross-border collaboration, and promoting global mobility. A workforce that is globally aware and culturally sensitive is better equipped to execute a global strategy.

7. Monitor, Evaluate, and Adapt: The global business environment is dynamic, with rapid changes in markets, competition, and regulations. Continuously monitor global operations against performance metrics and be prepared to adapt your strategy in response to new insights and challenges. This agility can provide a competitive edge, allowing your organization to capitalize on emerging opportunities and navigate global risks.

Developing and implementing a global strategy is a complex but rewarding endeavor. It requires a careful balance between global aspirations and local execution, all underpinned by a deep commitment to understanding and adapting to the nuances of international markets. By following these guidelines, organizations can align their global strategy with their vision, harness international opportunities, and achieve sustainable growth on the world stage.

Integrating global leadership competencies into a personal development plan involves a strategic approach to enhancing one's ability to lead effectively across cultures, stay informed of global trends, and expand international networks. This process enables leaders to navigate the complexities of the global business landscape with confidence and insight. Here is a structured method for incorporating these essential skills into your leadership development journey.

Start with a self-assessment to identify your current strengths and areas for improvement in relation to global leadership competencies. Consider your level of cultural intelligence, awareness of global trends impacting your industry, and the extent of your international network. This reflective exercise sets the foundation for targeted development efforts.

Set specific, measurable goals for enhancing your global leadership competencies. These goals might include increasing your cultural intelligence score, actively participating in global industry forums, or expanding your international network by a certain number. Clear goals provide direction and focus for your development activities.

Develop cultural intelligence by engaging in cross-cultural training programs, learning new languages, or participating in cultural immersion experiences. Emphasize understanding and appreciating diverse perspectives, communication styles, and business practices. This knowledge enhances your ability to connect with and lead people from different cultural backgrounds.

Stay informed of global trends by curating a list of reliable sources for international business news, subscribing to industry-specific publications, and attending global conferences. Allocate regular time in your schedule to absorb and reflect on this information, considering its implications for your organization and leadership approach.

Expand your international network by identifying key regions or countries relevant to your industry and leadership goals. Leverage professional networking platforms, join international industry associations, and attend global events to connect with peers and thought leaders from these areas. Focus on building genuine relationships that offer mutual value and learning opportunities.

Implement strategies for applying new insights and skills in your current role. This might involve leading a cross-cultural project team, initiating a global market analysis for your organization, or mentoring emerging leaders from different parts of the world. Practical application solidifies learning and demonstrates your growing global leadership competencies.

Seek feedback from mentors, peers, and team members with diverse cultural backgrounds on your progress in developing global leadership competencies. This feedback provides valuable insights into your effectiveness and areas needing further development.

Regularly review and adjust your personal development plan based on feedback and changing global business dynamics. This iterative process ensures your growth efforts remain relevant and aligned with your leadership goals.

Incorporating global leadership competencies into your personal development plan is a dynamic and ongoing process. By systematically enhancing your cultural intelligence, staying abreast of global trends, and expanding your international network, you equip yourself with the skills necessary to lead successfully in the global arena. This commitment to personal and professional growth not only advances your leadership capabilities but also contributes to the global success of your organization.

Measuring growth in global leadership competencies is essential for understanding the effectiveness of your development efforts and ensuring your skills remain aligned with the demands of the global business landscape. This process requires a multifaceted approach, incorporating self-assessment, feedback, and reflection to gauge progress and make necessary adjustments to your development plan.

Begin by establishing clear benchmarks at the outset of your global leadership development journey. These benchmarks should be based on the specific competencies you aim to develop, such as cultural intelligence, understanding of global trends, and the breadth of your international network. Having clear, measurable goals allows you to track your progress over time and provides a baseline for assessment.

Regular self-assessment is a vital component of measuring growth. Periodically review your goals and evaluate your current level of competence against the benchmarks you set. Consider using formal assessment tools or questionnaires designed to measure aspects of global leadership, such as cultural intelligence scales or global mindset inventories. This self-assessment process helps identify areas of improvement and reinforces your commitment to continuous learning.

Feedback from peers, mentors, and team members, particularly those from diverse cultural backgrounds or international markets, offers invaluable insights into your global leadership effectiveness. Encourage honest and constructive feedback on your communication style, decision-making, and ability to navigate cross-cultural interactions. This external perspective can highlight strengths and pinpoint areas that may not be apparent through self-assessment alone.

Reflection on real-world experiences is another crucial technique for measuring global leadership growth. Analyze specific instances where you applied your global leadership competencies, such as leading a multicultural team, negotiating an international partnership, or adapting business strategies to new markets. Reflect on the outcomes of these experiences, what you learned, and how you could improve in future similar situations.

In addition to these assessment methods, actively seek opportunities to showcase your global leadership competencies in professional settings. Taking on leadership roles in international projects, contributing to global strategy discussions, or participating in cross-cultural training initiatives can provide practical evidence of your growth and effectiveness as a global leader.

Based on the outcomes of your assessments, feedback, and reflections, adjust your development plan as necessary. The global business environment is continuously evolving, and your growth strategy should be flexible enough to adapt to new challenges and opportunities. This might involve focusing on new areas of development, seeking additional resources or experiences, or revising your goals to align with changing dynamics.

Measuring growth in global leadership competencies requires a structured yet adaptable approach. By combining self-assessment, soliciting feedback, reflecting on practical experiences, and continuously adjusting your development plan, you can ensure sustained progress in your journey as a global leader. This ongoing process not only enhances your ability to lead effectively across cultures and markets but also positions you to make a significant impact in the global business arena.

In concluding our exploration of global executive leadership, we underscore the critical importance of cultural intelligence, an acute awareness of global trends, and strategic approaches to expanding influence on the international stage. These pillars form the bedrock of effective global leadership, enabling leaders to navigate the complexities of the international business landscape with insight, empathy, and agility.

Cultural intelligence stands out as a fundamental competency, allowing leaders to bridge diverse cultural divides, foster inclusive work environments, and lead multinational teams with sensitivity and understanding. The ability to appreciate and leverage cultural diversity is not just a moral imperative but a strategic advantage in today's globalized economy.

Similarly, a keen awareness of global trends — from technological advancements to shifts in economic power and pressing sustainability challenges — equips leaders with the foresight needed to steer their organizations through turbulent waters. Understanding these dynamics enables leaders to anticipate changes, seize opportunities, and mitigate risks, ensuring their organizations remain competitive and resilient.

Strategies for expanding global influence are essential for leaders aiming to make an impact beyond their local markets. This involves not only building and leveraging international networks but also embodying a global mindset in decision-making and strategy formulation. Leaders who successfully project their vision and values on the global stage can drive significant growth and innovation for their organizations.

To enhance these global leadership capabilities, we encourage readers to actively engage with the exercises provided throughout this exploration. These practical steps are designed to build cultural intelligence, deepen understanding of global trends, and refine strategies for international influence. By applying these insights, leaders can further develop their skills and expand their impact in a global context.

It's essential to recognize that the journey of global executive leadership development is ongoing. The rapid pace of change in the global business environment demands continuous learning, adaptability, and a steadfast commitment to global mindedness. Leaders must remain curious, open to new experiences, and dedicated to personal and professional growth. Embracing this journey with enthusiasm and resilience will not only enhance a leader's effectiveness but also contribute to the broader mission of fostering global understanding and cooperation.

The path to global executive leadership is marked by challenges and opportunities in equal measure. By prioritizing cultural intelligence, staying attuned to global trends, and strategically expanding their influence, leaders can navigate these complexities successfully. The journey is demanding, yet immensely rewarding, offering the chance to make a lasting impact on the global stage. With commitment, perseverance, and an openness to continuous learning, leaders can thrive in this dynamic role, shaping not only the future of their organizations but also contributing to a more interconnected and understanding world.

Exercises for Chapter 9: Global Executive Leadership Coaching

Exercise 23: Cultural Intelligence Quiz

This quiz is designed to help you assess your current level of cultural intelligence (CQ) and understand how cultural diversity impacts leadership and team dynamics. Answer the questions honestly to gain insights into your strengths and areas for improvement.

Part 1: Self-Assessment Questions

1. How often do you interact with individuals from cultures different from your own?

2. Rate your comfort level when working in culturally diverse teams.

3. How frequently do you seek out information or resources to learn about other cultures?

4. Assess your ability to adapt your communication style to suit different cultural contexts.

5. Reflect on a recent multicultural interaction. Were you able to accurately interpret non-verbal cues?

Scoring for Part 1: For questions 1, 3, and 5, give yourself 0 points for rarely, 1 point for sometimes, and 2 points for often. For questions 2 and 4, give yourself 0 points for uncomfortable, 1 point for moderately comfortable, and 2 points for very comfortable.

Part 2: Reflection Questions

1. Think of a time when a cultural misunderstanding occurred within your team. What was the misunderstanding, and how was it resolved?

2. Reflect on the diverse cultural backgrounds of your team members. How do these differences enhance the team's creativity and problem-solving abilities?

3. Consider a leadership decision you made that was influenced by your cultural background. How might someone from a different culture have approached the decision differently?

4. Identify a cultural norm from another culture that you find challenging to understand. How might learning more about this norm improve your leadership effectiveness?

5. Envision leading a team in a country other than your own. What aspects of your leadership style would you need to adapt to be effective?

Scoring for Part 2:

There are no right or wrong answers in Part 2. Instead, use your responses as a guide to areas where you could enhance your cultural understanding and adaptability.

Results: If your score in Part 1 is 8-10, you likely have a high level of cultural intelligence but should continue to develop this skill. A score of 4-7 suggests a moderate level of cultural intelligence, with room for growth in understanding and adapting to cultural diversity. Scores 0-3 indicate an area for significant development. Consider engaging more deeply with cultures different from your own.

Next Steps: Based on your quiz results and reflections, identify specific actions you can take to enhance your cultural intelligence.

This might include learning a new language, participating in cultural exchange programs, or simply expanding your network to include more diverse contacts. Remember, improving your CQ is a continuous journey that enriches both your personal growth and your effectiveness as a leader in a globalized world.

Exercise 24: Global Leadership Challenge Case Study

This interactive case study revolves around a global leadership challenge faced by "TechGlobal," a fictional multinational technology firm planning to expand its operations into Southeast Asia. The company, known for its innovative products in the Western market, encounters significant cultural, regulatory, and market-entry challenges. As the newly appointed head of the Southeast Asian expansion, you are tasked with navigating these complexities to ensure a successful launch.

TechGlobal has developed a cutting-edge software solution that has seen tremendous success in North American and European markets. The company's leadership believes this product can solve many issues faced by businesses in Southeast Asia. However, preliminary research indicates several potential barriers:

- Cultural Differences: The product's user interface and marketing materials, designed with Western consumers in mind, may not resonate with Southeast Asian cultural norms and values.

- Regulatory Hurdles: Each country within Southeast Asia has its own set of regulations regarding data privacy and technology products, which are markedly different from those in the West.

- Market Entry Strategy: TechGlobal needs to decide whether to enter the market directly, form local partnerships, or adopt a franchise model, considering the pros and cons of each approach in light of local business practices.

Analyze the given situation and develop a comprehensive strategy addressing the following aspects:

1. Cultural Adaptation: Propose modifications to the product and marketing strategy that align with Southeast Asian cultural norms and consumer preferences.

2. Regulatory Compliance: Outline a plan for navigating the regulatory landscape in the region, ensuring the product meets all legal requirements.

3. Market Entry: Recommend an entry strategy that balances TechGlobal's strengths with local market dynamics, including potential partnerships or alliances.

Group Discussion or Reflection Prompts:

1. Cultural Sensitivity: How can TechGlobal ensure its product and marketing strategies are culturally sensitive and appealing to the Southeast Asian market?

2. Stakeholder Engagement: What steps should TechGlobal take to engage local stakeholders (e.g., government officials, business partners, consumers) in its expansion strategy?

3. Leadership Adaptability: As a leader, how would you adapt your leadership style to manage a multicultural team tasked with this expansion? Discuss the importance of cultural intelligence in this scenario.

4. Learning from Global Brands: Can you think of global brands that have successfully entered Southeast Asian markets? What lessons can TechGlobal learn from these cases?

5. Long-term Sustainability: Beyond the initial market entry, what should TechGlobal do to ensure the long-term sustainability of its operations in Southeast Asia?

This case study challenges you to apply global leadership principles to real-world scenarios, testing your ability to think strategically, navigate cultural and regulatory complexities, and lead effectively across borders. Reflecting on these prompts and discussing potential solutions will enhance your understanding of global leadership challenges and prepare you for similar situations in your professional journey.

Exercise 25: Reflective Journaling on Key Takeaways and Personal

This exercise is designed to encourage deep reflection on the key insights gained from your exploration of executive leadership and to articulate a personal growth plan based on these takeaways. Reflective journaling is a powerful tool for consolidating learning, fostering self-awareness, and setting actionable goals for continued development.

Step 1: Key Insights Reflection

Dedicate a quiet moment to reflect on the most impactful insights you've gained regarding executive leadership. Consider the concepts of emotional intelligence, strategic thinking, cultural intelligence, global leadership competencies, and the psychological aspects of leadership. Write down the insights that resonated with you the most and why they hold significance in your personal and professional life.

Step 2: Self-Assessment

Reflect on your current leadership practices and how they align with the concepts and strategies discussed. Identify areas where you excel and areas where there is room for improvement. Be honest and objective in your assessment, recognizing both your strengths and opportunities for growth.

Step 3: Personal Growth Goals

Based on your reflections and self-assessment, define specific personal growth goals. These goals should be SMART (Specific, Measurable, Achievable, Relevant, Time-bound) and aligned with enhancing your leadership capabilities. For each goal, identify why it's important to you and how it will contribute to your effectiveness as a leader.

Step 4: Action Plan

For each personal growth goal, outline a detailed action plan. This plan should include the steps you will take to achieve the goal, resources you might need (such as books, courses, or mentors), and a timeline for completion. Consider how you will integrate these actions into your daily routine and how you will measure progress.

Step 5: Anticipating Challenges

Anticipate potential challenges you might face in pursuing your personal growth goals and strategize how to overcome them. This could involve time management issues, resistance to change, or external obstacles. Planning for these challenges in advance can help you navigate them more effectively when they arise.

Step 6: Commitment to Continuous Learning

Conclude your journaling exercise with a commitment to continuous learning and adaptation. Acknowledge that leadership development is an ongoing journey and that the landscape of executive leadership will continue to evolve. Write down how you plan to stay informed, remain open to new ideas, and continue refining your leadership skills over time.

Step 7: Regular Review and Adjustment

Commit to regularly reviewing your journal entries, personal growth goals, and action plans. Set a schedule for this review process, whether it's monthly, quarterly, or bi-annually. Use these reviews as opportunities to assess progress, celebrate achievements, and make necessary adjustments to your goals and plans.

Reflective journaling on key takeaways and crafting a personal growth plan is a proactive step towards becoming a more effective, insightful, and adaptive leader. By engaging in this exercise, you solidify your learning, set a clear direction for your development, and prepare yourself to meet the challenges and opportunities of executive leadership with confidence and skill.

Conclusion

As we approach the conclusion of our exploration into executive leadership, it's imperative to reflect on the foundational concepts that have shaped our understanding and approach to this complex and dynamic field. This book has delved into the multifaceted nature of executive leadership, underscoring the critical importance of emotional intelligence, strategic thinking, and the psychological underpinnings that influence leadership effectiveness and organizational success.

At the heart of effective executive leadership lies a deep understanding of oneself and others, a concept that we've explored through the lens of emotional intelligence. Recognizing and managing one's own emotions, while empathetically navigating the emotions of others, is crucial for building strong relationships, fostering a positive organizational culture, and leading teams to achieve their highest potential. Emotional intelligence serves as the cornerstone for effective communication, conflict resolution, and motivation, enabling leaders to guide their organizations with wisdom and compassion.

Strategic thinking has been another key theme, emphasizing the need for leaders to look beyond the immediate challenges to envision and plan for the future. This involves a careful analysis of the competitive landscape, an understanding of global trends, and the ability to innovate and adapt strategies to meet evolving market demands. Strategic thinking empowers leaders to make informed decisions that drive long-term success, ensuring their organizations remain resilient and competitive in an ever-changing business environment.

We've examined the psychological underpinnings of leadership, including the impact of leadership styles on team dynamics, the importance of mindset in overcoming challenges, and the role of resilience in sustaining leadership effectiveness. Understanding these psychological aspects allows leaders to better navigate the complexities of human behavior, leading to more effective and impactful leadership practices.

Throughout this book, the aim has been to provide insights and strategies that equip current and aspiring executive leaders with the knowledge and skills necessary to lead with confidence, integrity, and foresight. By embracing the principles of emotional intelligence, strategic thinking, and psychological insight, leaders can inspire and guide their teams toward achieving shared goals and fostering organizational excellence.

It's important to recognize that the journey of leadership development is ongoing. The landscape of executive leadership is continually evolving, demanding a commitment to lifelong learning, self-reflection, and adaptation. The concepts and strategies discussed in this book are intended to serve as a foundation upon which leaders can build and refine their skills, navigating the challenges and opportunities of leadership with grace and resilience.

Throughout this exploration of executive leadership, a range of coaching strategies and techniques have been highlighted, each designed to impact leadership development profoundly. These approaches encompass feedback mechanisms, time management practices, and the cultivation of a continuous learning culture, among others. By integrating these techniques, leaders can enhance their effectiveness, adaptability, and resilience, ensuring they are well-equipped to navigate the complexities of the modern business environment.

Feedback mechanisms stand out as a critical component of leadership development. Constructive feedback, whether it's peer-to-peer, from subordinates, or from mentors, provides leaders with valuable insights into their performance, communication style, and decision-making processes. Such feedback not only illuminates areas for improvement but also reinforces strengths, facilitating a more self-aware and reflective approach to leadership.

Time management practices are another key area of focus. Effective leaders must master the art of prioritizing tasks, delegating responsibilities, and managing their time to balance the demands of their roles. Techniques such as setting clear goals, breaking tasks into manageable steps, and using tools to track progress can significantly enhance productivity and reduce stress. Leaders who excel in time management are better positioned to focus on strategic initiatives and personal development activities.

The cultivation of a continuous learning culture within organizations is also emphasized as a pivotal coaching strategy. Leaders play a crucial role in fostering an environment that values curiosity, innovation, and ongoing professional growth. By encouraging team members to pursue learning opportunities, share knowledge, and experiment with new ideas, leaders can drive organizational success and adaptability. This culture of learning not only supports the individual development of team members but also ensures the organization as a whole remains responsive to changing market dynamics and technological advancements.

In addition to these core areas, effective coaching techniques also involve the development of emotional intelligence, strategic thinking capabilities, and cultural competence. Emotional intelligence enhances leaders' ability to connect with others, navigate complex interpersonal dynamics, and lead with empathy. Strategic thinking empowers leaders to anticipate future challenges and opportunities, developing forward-looking strategies that ensure long-term success. Cultural competence, particularly in a globalized business context, enables leaders to effectively manage diverse teams and leverage the strengths of a multicultural workforce.

The coaching strategies and techniques detailed throughout this book are essential tools for any leader seeking to enhance their leadership development. By focusing on feedback mechanisms, time management, continuous learning, and other key areas, leaders can build a solid foundation for their growth and success. These approaches not only benefit the individual leader but also have a profound impact on their teams and organizations, driving performance, innovation, and resilience in an ever-evolving business landscape.

The transformative journey of leadership coaching unfolds through a series of insights, practices, and challenges that fundamentally reshape an executive's approach to leadership. This reflection delves into the profound impact of leadership coaching, the critical role of executive presence and branding, and the nuanced landscape of global leadership in today's culturally diverse and rapidly evolving business environment.

Leadership coaching emerges as a powerful catalyst for transformation, providing leaders with the tools, perspectives, and feedback necessary to unlock their potential. It facilitates a deeper understanding of one's strengths and weaknesses, encouraging introspection and personal growth. Through targeted coaching, leaders develop the agility to navigate complex situations, enhance their decision-making skills, and refine their ability to inspire and influence others. This process is not just about acquiring new skills but about fostering a mindset of continuous improvement and resilience.

The concept of executive presence and personal branding stands at the core of effective leadership. Executive presence, encompassing a leader's ability to command respect, communicate with clarity, and exhibit confidence, is pivotal in establishing credibility and inspiring confidence among peers, stakeholders, and teams. Personal branding, meanwhile, allows leaders to articulate their unique value proposition, aligning their professional identity with their leadership vision and values. Together, executive presence and personal branding create a powerful narrative that distinguishes a leader, enabling them to leave a lasting impact on their organization and industry.

Global leadership presents a distinct set of challenges and opportunities, accentuated by the richness of cultural diversity and the pace of change in the global business landscape. Leading across cultures demands a high degree of cultural intelligence, including the ability to respect, understand, and leverage cultural differences to foster collaboration and innovation. Global leaders must also stay attuned to worldwide trends, adapting their strategies to meet shifting economic, technological, and social dynamics. This global perspective is crucial for identifying opportunities for growth, navigating international markets, and leading diverse, geographically dispersed teams.

The opportunities that arise from global leadership are as significant as the challenges. Leaders who successfully navigate the complexities of the global environment can drive their organizations to new heights, tapping into emerging markets, fostering global partnerships, and cultivating a richly diverse and innovative organizational culture. The ability to lead with a global mindset, embracing diversity and leveraging the interconnectedness of the world, becomes a key differentiator in achieving sustainable success.

The journey of leadership transformation, underscored by the development of executive presence, personal branding, and global leadership competencies, is both challenging and rewarding. It requires leaders to engage in continuous learning, adapt to the rapid changes of the global business environment, and navigate the complexities of cultural diversity with empathy and insight. As leaders embark on this transformative journey, they not only enhance their capability to lead effectively but also contribute to building organizations that are resilient, innovative, and globally competitive. This reflection underscores the importance of embracing transformation, diversity, and global mindedness as essential elements of contemporary leadership.

The future of executive leadership and coaching is poised to unfold against a backdrop of rapid technological advancements, shifting global dynamics, and evolving societal expectations. This evolving landscape demands a reimagined approach to leadership, where adaptability, innovation, and resilience become paramount. As we look ahead, several anticipated trends are likely to shape the contours of executive leadership and coaching.

The digital transformation continues to be a significant driver of change, pushing leaders to not only embrace new technologies but also to lead their organizations through digital transitions. This requires a deep understanding of digital trends, from artificial intelligence and machine learning to blockchain and the Internet of Things. Leaders must leverage these technologies to drive efficiency, innovation, and competitive advantage, all while managing the cybersecurity risks and ethical considerations they entail.

Sustainability and social responsibility are moving to the forefront of business strategy, reflecting a growing recognition of the urgent need to address climate change, resource scarcity, and social inequalities. Future leaders will be expected to integrate sustainability into the core of their business models, making decisions that balance profit with environmental stewardship and social well-being. This shift necessitates a long-term perspective and a commitment to ethical leadership.

The increasing complexity of the global business environment, marked by geopolitical tensions, economic volatility, and cultural diversity, calls for leaders with a global mindset. They must be adept at navigating international markets, understanding cultural nuances, and leading diverse, geographically dispersed teams. Success in this arena requires a sophisticated appreciation of global interconnectivity and the ability to think and act strategically across borders.

The future of work is characterized by evolving work arrangements, including remote and hybrid models, necessitating a reevaluation of traditional leadership and management practices. Leaders must find new ways to foster team cohesion, maintain productivity, and ensure employee well-being in a distributed work environment. This will involve harnessing digital tools for collaboration and communication, as well as developing skills in virtual leadership and team building.

The role of emotional intelligence in leadership is becoming increasingly recognized as vital for navigating the complexities of the modern workplace. Leaders must possess the empathy, self-awareness, and social skills to lead with compassion, build strong relationships, and manage the emotional dynamics of their teams. As such, coaching programs will likely place greater emphasis on developing these emotional competencies alongside strategic and operational skills.

In response to these trends, executive coaching will evolve to support leaders in developing the agility to navigate change, the creativity to drive innovation, and the resilience to withstand challenges. Coaching will become more personalized, leveraging data and technology to provide insights into individual strengths and areas for growth. Additionally, there will be a greater focus on coaching for sustainability leadership, digital transformation, and global strategy, reflecting the changing priorities of the business world.

The future of executive leadership and coaching is marked by the need for adaptability, innovation, and resilience. Leaders who embrace these imperatives, continuously develop their skills, and align their practices with emerging trends will be well-positioned to lead their organizations to success in an increasingly complex and dynamic global landscape.

The evolving landscape of executive leadership, characterized by rapid technological change, global interconnectedness, and an increased emphasis on sustainability, necessitates a corresponding evolution in executive coaching. As these trends continue to shape the business environment, coaching is expected to adapt by placing a greater focus on fostering global competencies, digital fluency, and sustainability awareness among leaders.

Executive coaching will increasingly aim to develop leaders who are not just proficient in navigating the complexities of the global market but are also culturally intelligent and capable of leading diverse, international teams. This involves cultivating an understanding of cultural nuances, communication styles, and business practices across different regions. Coaches will employ strategies that encourage leaders to engage with and learn from a variety of cultural perspectives, enhancing their ability to make informed decisions that respect and leverage global diversity.

Digital fluency is becoming a critical competency for leaders, given the centrality of digital transformation across industries. Executive coaching will place a premium on helping leaders understand and leverage emerging technologies that impact their business. This doesn't mean turning leaders into technology experts but rather ensuring they possess the knowledge to make strategic decisions about technology investments, cybersecurity, and digital innovation. Coaching will also support leaders in managing the human side of digital transformation, including leading change initiatives and fostering a culture of digital agility within their organizations.

Sustainability awareness is another area where executive coaching is expected to evolve significantly. Coaches will work with leaders to integrate sustainability into their strategic thinking and decision-making processes. This involves understanding the environmental, social, and governance (ESG) factors that impact business operations and the broader community. Leaders will be encouraged to think beyond short-term profit to consider the long-term impact of their decisions on the planet and society. Coaching will support leaders in navigating the complex trade-offs involved in pursuing sustainability goals, helping them to align their business strategies with sustainable development principles.

Executive coaching will increasingly utilize technology to enhance the coaching experience. From data analytics and AI-driven insights to virtual reality and online platforms, technology will enable more personalized, flexible, and accessible coaching interventions. This will allow coaching to be more tailored to the individual needs of leaders, providing them with targeted support as they navigate the challenges of leadership in a rapidly changing world.

In response to these trends, executive coaching will also emphasize the importance of resilience, emotional intelligence, and lifelong learning. Coaches will work with leaders to develop the personal and professional qualities needed to lead with empathy, adapt to unforeseen challenges, and remain committed to continuous improvement. By focusing on these areas, executive coaching will prepare leaders not just to succeed in the current environment but to thrive in the future landscape of business.

As the demands on leaders continue to evolve, so too will the role of coaching in leadership development. By focusing on global competencies, digital fluency, sustainability awareness, and the personal qualities essential for effective leadership, executive coaching will play a pivotal role in shaping the leaders of the future—leaders who are adaptable, innovative, and prepared to address the complex challenges and opportunities of the 21st century.

The journey of leadership and coaching is inherently marked by continuous improvement, learning, and adaptation. In the rapidly evolving landscape of global business, the only constant is change, making it imperative for leaders and coaches alike to remain committed to their own development. This commitment ensures not only personal and professional growth but also the ability to lead effectively and make a positive impact in an ever-changing environment.

Leadership is not a static achievement but a dynamic process that evolves with each new challenge and opportunity. As such, continuous learning is crucial. The most effective leaders are those who remain curious and open-minded, actively seeking new knowledge, skills, and experiences. This approach allows them to stay ahead of industry trends, anticipate future challenges, and lead their organizations with foresight and agility.

Similarly, self-reflection is an essential component of the leadership journey. It involves taking the time to consider not only what you have achieved but how you have achieved it. Reflecting on your experiences, decisions, and their outcomes provides valuable insights into your leadership style, strengths, and areas for improvement. It is through this process of self-examination that leaders can deepen their self-awareness and refine their approach to leadership.

Adaptation, too, is key to sustaining effective leadership and coaching practices. The ability to adapt to new situations, challenges, and information allows leaders and coaches to remain relevant and effective. This might involve changing leadership styles to better suit a new team dynamic, revising strategies in response to shifting market conditions, or adopting new technologies to enhance productivity and innovation.

For coaches, the journey of continuous improvement involves staying abreast of the latest theories, tools, and techniques in coaching practice. It also means reflecting on their coaching interactions and outcomes to learn and grow from each experience. By doing so, coaches can provide more impactful guidance and support to the leaders they work with, helping them navigate their own journeys of development.

The importance of building a supportive network cannot be overstressed. Surrounding yourself with mentors, peers, and professionals who challenge and inspire you can provide the encouragement and feedback necessary for growth. These relationships offer diverse perspectives and insights, enriching your understanding and approach to leadership and coaching.

Leadership and coaching are journeys of continuous improvement that demand lifelong learning, self-reflection, and the ability to adapt. By embracing these principles, leaders and coaches can enhance their effectiveness, navigate the complexities of the modern world, and lead with confidence and insight. The journey is both challenging and rewarding, offering endless opportunities for growth and impact. It is a path that requires persistence, resilience, and an unwavering commitment to excellence, but the rewards—for the individual, their team, and their organization—are immeasurable.

Maintaining a growth mindset is essential for lifelong learning, ensuring that leaders continue to evolve and remain effective in an ever-changing environment. This mindset fosters openness to new experiences, resilience in the face of challenges, and a constant pursuit of knowledge. Here are strategies for cultivating and sustaining a growth mindset throughout your professional journey.

Embracing new challenges is a cornerstone of lifelong learning. Actively seek opportunities that push you out of your comfort zone, whether that's taking on a project outside of your usual scope, stepping into a new leadership role, or tackling a problem with no clear solution. These experiences not only build new skills but also enhance your ability to adapt and innovate.

Staying informed about industry trends is another critical strategy. The business landscape is continuously evolving, with new technologies, methodologies, and market dynamics emerging regularly. Dedicate time to reading industry publications, attending conferences, and participating in workshops. This commitment keeps you at the forefront of your field, ready to leverage new opportunities and address emerging challenges.

Engaging in professional networks and communities offers invaluable opportunities for learning and development. These networks provide access to a wealth of knowledge, diverse perspectives, and support. They can be a source of inspiration, a sounding board for ideas, and a resource for solutions to challenges. Participate actively in professional associations, online forums, and networking events. Share your experiences and learn from the successes and failures of others.

Reflecting on your experiences is a powerful learning tool. Regularly take stock of your achievements, the obstacles you've encountered, and the lessons learned along the way. This reflection not only consolidates your learning but also provides insights into how you can improve and grow further. Journaling, mentoring, and coaching can facilitate this reflective practice.

Setting personal and professional development goals ensures your growth remains focused and purposeful. Identify specific areas where you want to improve or new skills you wish to acquire. Create actionable plans to achieve these goals, incorporating timelines and milestones. Regularly review and adjust these goals as your career evolves and new learning needs emerge.

Fostering a culture of learning within your organization amplifies your growth mindset. Encourage curiosity, experimentation, and knowledge sharing among your team. By leading by example and supporting others in their development, you create an environment where continuous learning is valued and practiced by all.

Maintaining a growth mindset through lifelong learning is crucial for leadership success. By embracing new challenges, staying informed about industry trends, engaging in professional networks, reflecting on experiences, setting development goals, and fostering a learning culture, leaders can ensure they continue to grow and thrive in their careers. This proactive approach to learning not only enriches the leader's professional journey but also enhances their capacity to lead effectively and make a positive impact.

Developing a personal growth plan is a strategic process that involves self-reflection, goal setting, and action planning. It's a way to translate the insights gained from your leadership and coaching experiences into a structured path for further development. Here's how to create an effective personal growth plan:

Start with a thorough self-assessment to identify your strengths and areas for improvement. Reflect on feedback received from peers, mentors, and team members, as well as your own observations of your leadership and coaching practices. Consider areas such as emotional intelligence, strategic thinking, communication skills, cultural competence, and adaptability.

Define specific, measurable goals based on your self-assessment. These goals should address both your areas for improvement and your aspirations to expand your leadership and coaching competencies. Be clear about what success looks like for each goal and set realistic timelines for achieving them.

Identify the resources and actions required to achieve your goals. This may include enrolling in leadership development programs, seeking out mentoring or coaching opportunities, attending workshops or conferences, reading specific books, or practicing new skills in your daily work. Allocate time in your schedule for these activities to ensure they receive the attention they deserve.

Establish metrics for tracking your progress. Depending on your goals, these could include qualitative feedback from others, self-rating scales on specific competencies, or quantitative measures such as completion of training programs or achievement of performance milestones.

Create a support system to help you achieve your goals. This could involve identifying a mentor or coach who can provide guidance and feedback, joining a professional network or community of practice, or forming a peer support group with colleagues who are also committed to personal development.

Regularly review and adjust your personal growth plan. Set aside time periodically to assess your progress toward your goals, reflect on what you've learned, and make any necessary adjustments to your plan. This iterative process allows you to respond to new challenges and opportunities that arise, ensuring your development efforts remain relevant and targeted.

Incorporate reflection and learning into your routine. Make it a habit to reflect on your experiences, successes, and failures, extracting lessons that can inform your future actions and decisions. Cultivating a mindset of continuous learning and curiosity will fuel your ongoing development and adaptation as a leader and coach.

By following these steps, you can create a personal growth plan that not only focuses on improving specific leadership and coaching competencies but also aligns with your broader professional aspirations. Such a plan ensures that you remain proactive in your development, poised to meet the demands of your role, and capable of making a meaningful impact in your organization and beyond.

As we reach the conclusion of this exploration into the realms of leadership and coaching, it's essential to recognize the transformative power these disciplines hold. The journey through the intricacies of executive leadership, the nuances of coaching, and the challenges of navigating the global business landscape reveals a path that is both demanding and deeply rewarding. At the core of this journey is the understanding that leadership and coaching are not merely about achieving business outcomes but about fostering growth, resilience, and positive change within individuals and organizations.

The dedication required to excel in leadership and coaching cannot be understated. It demands a commitment to continuous learning, an openness to feedback, and a willingness to adapt and evolve. This dedication is what fuels the ongoing development of leadership competencies, the deepening of emotional intelligence, and the cultivation of a global mindset. It is also what enables leaders and coaches to navigate the complexities of today's ever-changing business environment with confidence and competence.

Empathy emerges as a critical element in this journey. The ability to understand and share the feelings of others is fundamental to building strong, trusting relationships, fostering a culture of inclusivity, and leading with compassion. Empathy allows leaders and coaches to connect with people on a deeper level, enhancing their ability to motivate, inspire, and guide others toward their fullest potential. In the context of global leadership, empathy also facilitates cross-cultural understanding and collaboration, bridging divides and uniting teams across geographical and cultural boundaries.

Ethical practice stands as a pillar of effective leadership and coaching. In the pursuit of excellence, leaders and coaches must navigate ethical dilemmas and make decisions that reflect integrity, responsibility, and a commitment to doing what is right. Upholding ethical standards is essential for maintaining trust, credibility, and respect among peers, clients, and the broader community. It ensures that the pursuit of success is balanced with considerations of fairness, sustainability, and the well-being of all stakeholders.

The transformative power of leadership and coaching lies in their capacity to effect positive change—change that enhances individual lives, propels organizations forward, and contributes to the betterment of society. The journey of leadership and coaching is one of dedication, empathy, and ethical practice, driven by the relentless pursuit of excellence. As we move forward, let us carry these principles with us, guiding our actions and shaping our approach to the challenges and opportunities that lie ahead. The path to excellence is a journey of continuous growth and learning, and it is one that we embark on with the knowledge that our efforts can and will make a difference.

As we close this chapter on the exploration of leadership and coaching, it's not merely an end but a beginning—the start of your continued journey in the vast and dynamic realm of executive leadership. The principles and strategies discussed within these pages are more than just concepts; they are tools, waiting to be wielded by you in the pursuit of excellence in leadership and coaching. Now, the real work begins.

I urge you, the reader, to take these insights off the page and into your practice. Apply the principles of emotional intelligence in your interactions, employ strategic thinking in your decision-making, and weave the fabric of cultural intelligence into the tapestry of your leadership. Challenge yourself to embrace the continuous learning, self-reflection, and adaptation that define the most effective leaders and coaches.

The road ahead is replete with challenges but remember, within every challenge lies opportunity—an opportunity to grow, to inspire, and to lead change. Your role as an executive leader and coach places you in a unique position to influence not only the trajectory of your organization but the lives of the individuals you lead. Embrace this responsibility with dedication, empathy, and ethical practice.

Let the journey not intimidate you but invigorate you. The landscape of global business is ever-changing, demanding not just participation but leadership that is proactive, innovative, and resilient. As you move forward, carry with you the knowledge that leadership and coaching are not just about reaching destinations but about shaping journeys—yours and those of the people you lead.

So, I call upon you to take action. Implement the strategies outlined, engage with the exercises provided, and embark on a path of personal and professional development. Seek out new challenges, foster inclusivity, and strive for sustainability in all your endeavors. Let the principles of effective leadership and coaching guide you as you navigate the complexities of the executive role.

In the pursuit of excellence, remember that you are not alone. Surround yourself with mentors, peers, and a network of fellow leaders and coaches committed to growth and excellence. Share your experiences, learn from each other, and build a community of practice that supports continuous improvement and innovation.

The journey of executive leadership and coaching is one of profound impact and enduring significance. It is a journey marked by the power to transform—to transform yourself, your team, your organization, and ultimately, the world around you. Embrace this journey with courage, conviction, and an unwavering commitment to excellence. The future awaits, and it is yours to shape.

Appendices

Books

1. "Becoming a Resonant Leader: Develop Your Emotional Intelligence, Renew Your Relationships, Sustain Your Effectiveness" by Annie McKee, Richard Boyatzis, and Frances Johnston - This book delves into the importance of emotional intelligence in leadership and offers practical advice for developing resonance within teams.

2. "Co-Active Coaching: Changing Business, Transforming Lives" by Henry Kimsey-House, Karen Kimsey-House, Phillip Sandahl, and Laura Whitworth - Regarded as a seminal work in the field of coaching, it presents the co-active coaching model and its application in various contexts.

3. "Drive: The Surprising Truth About What Motivates Us" by Daniel H. Pink - Pink's exploration of motivation offers critical insights for leaders seeking to inspire and engage their teams more effectively.

4. "Emotional Intelligence: Why It Can Matter More Than IQ" by Daniel Goleman - A groundbreaking work that introduced the concept of emotional intelligence and its critical role in leadership.

5. "Good to Great: Why Some Companies Make the Leap and Others Don't" by Jim Collins - Collins provides a research-based analysis of what distinguishes top-performing companies from their competitors, offering valuable lessons for leaders.

6. "Leaders Eat Last: Why Some Teams Pull Together and Others Don't" by Simon Sinek - This book explores the role of leadership in creating environments where teams can thrive and succeed together.

7. "Leadership and Self-Deception: Getting Out of the Box" by The Arbinger Institute - Offers a unique perspective on leadership challenges and personal growth, focusing on the importance of overcoming self-deception.

8. "Mindset: The New Psychology of Success" by Carol S. Dweck - Dweck's concept of fixed and growth mindsets has profound implications for leadership, coaching, and personal development.

9. "Multipliers: How the Best Leaders Make Everyone Smarter" by Liz Wiseman - Explores how leaders can amplify the intelligence and capabilities of their teams, transforming organizational performance.

10. "The 7 Habits of Highly Effective People: Powerful Lessons in Personal Change" by Stephen R. Covey - A classic text on personal effectiveness that has informed leadership practices worldwide.

11. "The Coaching Habit: Say Less, Ask More & Change the Way You Lead Forever" by Michael Bungay Stanier - Provides simple yet powerful techniques for incorporating coaching into daily leadership.

12. "The Culture Code: The Secrets of Highly Successful Groups" by Daniel Coyle - Examines the group dynamics that drive successful organizations, offering insights into building strong, cohesive teams.

13. "The Fifth Discipline: The Art & Practice of The Learning Organization" by Peter M. Senge - Focuses on systems thinking and its application in creating organizations that excel at learning and adapting.

14. "The Leadership Challenge: How to Make Extraordinary Things Happen in Organizations" by James M. Kouzes and Barry Z. Posner - Offers evidence-based practices for effective leadership based on extensive research.

15. "Trillion Dollar Coach: The Leadership Playbook of Silicon Valley's Bill Campbell" by Eric Schmidt, Jonathan Rosenberg, and Alan Eagle - Shares the leadership principles and coaching philosophy of Bill Campbell, who played a pivotal role in the success of several major tech companies.

Academic Journals and Articles

- Academy of Management Journal: Offers comprehensive research on management and organizational concepts, including groundbreaking leadership studies.

- The Leadership Quarterly: An interdisciplinary journal dedicated to advancing the understanding of leadership as a phenomenon and its impact on organizations.

- Harvard Business Review: While not strictly an academic journal, it provides accessible, research-based articles on leadership and management practices from leading scholars and practitioners.

- Journal of Organizational Behavior: Publishes research on the dynamics of organizations and their management, with a focus on leadership and team dynamics.

- Coaching: An International Journal of Theory, Research and Practice: Focuses on bridging the gap between coaching practice and academic research, offering insights into effective coaching methodologies.

- Journal of Applied Psychology: Features empirical research on the application of psychological concepts to organizational settings, including leadership effectiveness and team dynamics.

- Leadership and Organization Development Journal: Provides a mix of theoretical and practical studies on leadership and its role in the development of organizations.

Seminal Articles:

- "Emotional intelligence" by Peter Salovey and John D. Mayer (1990): This foundational article introduced the concept of emotional intelligence and its relevance to understanding and managing emotions in oneself and others.

- "Leadership That Gets Results" by Daniel Goleman (Harvard Business Review, 2000): Goleman applies the concept of emotional intelligence to leadership, outlining six leadership styles and their effects on organizational climate and performance.

- "The Core Competencies of the Corporation" by C.K. Prahalad and Gary Hamel (Harvard Business Review, 1990): Though focused on strategic management, this article has implications for leadership in identifying and leveraging an organization's core competencies.

- "Inclusive Leadership: The View From Six Countries" by Jeanine Prime and Elizabeth R. Salib (Harvard Business Review, 2014): This article examines the impact of inclusive leadership on team innovation and performance across different cultural contexts.

- "Leadership behavior and employee voice: Is the door really open?" by James R. Detert and Amy C. Edmondson (Academy of Management Journal, 2011): Explores the dynamics between leadership behaviors and the willingness of employees to speak up or contribute ideas.

- "What Makes a Leader?" by Daniel Goleman (Harvard Business Review, 1998): Goleman discusses the role of emotional intelligence in effective leadership, arguing that it is as important, if not more so, than traditional measures of intelligence and technical skill.

- "Coaching with compassion versus coaching for compliance: Emotional and behavioral engagement in coach-coachee interactions" by Richard E. Boyatzis, Melvin L. Smith, and Ellen Van Oosten (Organizational Dynamics, 2019): This article contrasts two coaching approaches and their impact on coachee engagement and personal growth.

Online Resources

1. Harvard Business Review (HBR): Offers a wealth of articles, blogs, and podcasts on various aspects of leadership and management, authored by renowned academics and industry leaders. Its content is a blend of research-based insights and practical advice (https://hbr.org).

2. Forbes – Leadership: Features articles and commentary on the latest trends in leadership, organizational development, and career management, written by business leaders and experts (https://www.forbes.com/leadership/).

3. McKinsey Insights – Leadership: Provides in-depth articles and reports on leadership, organizational behavior, and corporate strategy, based on McKinsey & Company's extensive consulting experience and research (https://www.mckinsey.com/featured-insights/leadership).

4. The Leadership Circle: Offers resources and insights into leadership assessment and development. It's particularly known for its framework that integrates various leadership competencies and behaviors (https://leadershipcircle.com/en/).

5. International Coach Federation (ICF) Blog: As the leading global organization dedicated to advancing the coaching profession, ICF offers articles, research findings, and industry news on coaching practices and standards (https://coachingfederation.org/blog).

6. TED Talks – Leadership: Provides access to talks from some of the world's most innovative thinkers on topics related to leadership and management, offering both inspiration and practical advice (https://www.ted.com/topics/leadership).

7. Center for Creative Leadership (CCL): A top-ranked, global provider of leadership development and research, CCL offers articles, white papers, and reports on leadership development practices and strategies (https://www.ccl.org).

8. Coachfederation.org: Home of the International Coach Federation, it provides resources for professional coaches, including research, training programs, and standards of practice, as well as articles on coaching trends and methodologies.

9. Leadership Now: Features articles, blog posts, and book recommendations focused on building better leaders. It covers a wide range of topics, including ethical leadership, personal growth, and strategy (https://www.leadershipnow.com).

10. Switch & Shift: Offers content on the human side of business, including leadership, culture, and change management. It emphasizes ethical leadership and creating workplaces where employees thrive (https://switchandshift.com).

11. Marshall Goldsmith's Blog: Marshall Goldsmith, one of the world's leading executive coaches, shares insights on leadership development, coaching, and personal growth on his blog (https://www.marshallgoldsmith.com/blog/).